The
Wiersbe
BIBLE STUDY SERIES

The Wiersbe
BIBLE STUDY SERIES

MINOR PROPHETS
VOLUME 2

Demonstrating

Bravery by

Your Walk

DAVID C COOK

transforming lives together

THE WIERSBE BIBLE STUDY SERIES: MINOR PROPHETS (VOLUME 2)
Published by David C Cook
4050 Lee Vance Drive
Colorado Springs, CO 80918 U.S.A.

Integrity Music Limited, a Division of David C Cook
Brighton, East Sussex BN1 2RE, England

The graphic circle C logo is a registered trademark of David C Cook.

ISBN 978-1-4347-0695-9
eISBN 978-1-4347-0860-1

© 2014 Warren W. Wiersbe

The Team: Karen Lee-Thorp, Amy Konyndyk, Nick Lee, Jack
Campbell, Helen Macdonald, Karen Athen
Series Cover Design: John Hamilton Design
Cover Photo: Veer Images

Printed in the United States of America
First Edition 2014

2 3 4 5 6 7 8 9 10 11

011620

Contents

Introduction to Minor Prophets (Volume 2)

A Call for Heroes

Will Rogers once said, "We can't all be heroes because somebody has to sit on the curb and clap as they go by."

But we *can* all be heroes, at least from God's point of view, and that's far more important than the applause of the crowd on the curb. Those fifty thousand Jewish exiles who returned to Jerusalem to rebuild their temple and their lives were certainly heroes, the kind of heroes whose courage and sacrifice God's people today would do well to imitate. Their story is told in the Old Testament books of Ezra, Nehemiah, Haggai, and Zechariah. (See my separate Nehemiah study for more on that book.)

The Heroic Way

Ezra was a priest and Haggai and Zechariah were prophets, and together with Zerubbabel, the governor of Judah, they encouraged the Jewish remnant, overcame obstacles, and labored to finish the work God gave them to do.

"Most people aren't appreciated enough," wrote Peggy Noonan in *What I Saw at the Revolution*, "and the bravest things we do in our lives are

7

usually known only to ourselves. No one throws ticker tape on the man who chose to be faithful to his wife, on the lawyer who didn't take the drug money, or the daughter who held her tongue again and again. All this anonymous heroism" (Random, 2010, p. 253).

God is challenging us to be heroic in a world that desperately needs everyday anonymous heroes who will sacrifice and serve only to hear their Master say, "Well done!"

—*Warren W. Wiersbe*

How to Use This Study

This study is designed for both individual and small-group use. We've divided it into eight lessons—each references one or more chapters in Warren W. Wiersbe's commentary *Be Heroic* (second edition, David C Cook, 2010). While reading *Be Heroic* is not a prerequisite for going through this study, the additional insights and background Wiersbe offers can greatly enhance your study experience.

The **Getting Started** questions at the beginning of each lesson offer you an opportunity to record your first thoughts and reactions to the study text. This is an important step in the study process as those "first impressions" often include clues about what it is your heart is longing to discover.

The bulk of the study is found in the **Going Deeper** questions. These dive into the Bible text and, along with helpful excerpts from Wiersbe's commentary, help you examine not only the original context and meaning of the verses but also modern application.

Looking Inward narrows the focus down to your personal story. These intimate questions can be a bit uncomfortable at times, but don't shy away from honesty here. This is where you are asked to stand before the mirror of God's Word and look closely at what you see. It's the place to take a good look at yourself in light of the lesson and search for ways in which you can grow in faith.

Going Forward is the place where you can commit to paper those things you want or need to do in order to better live out the discoveries you made in the Looking Inward section. Don't skip or skim through this. Take the time to really consider what practical steps you might take to move closer to Christ. Then share your thoughts with a trusted friend who can act as an encourager and accountability partner.

Finally, there is a brief **Seeking Help** section to close the lesson. This is a reminder for you to invite God into your spiritual-growth process. If you choose to write out a prayer in this section, come back to it as you work through the lesson and continue to seek the Holy Spirit's guidance as you discover God's will for your life.

Tips for Small Groups

A small group is a dynamic thing. One week it might seem like a group of close-knit friends. The next it might seem more like a group of uncomfortable strangers. A small-group leader's role is to read these subtle changes and adjust the tone of the discussion accordingly.

Small groups need to be safe places for people to talk openly. It is through shared wrestling with difficult life issues that some of the greatest personal growth is discovered. But in order for the group to feel safe, participants need to know it's okay *not* to share sometimes. Always invite honest disclosure, but never force someone to speak if he or she isn't comfortable doing so. (A savvy leader will follow up later with a group member who isn't comfortable sharing in a group setting to see if a one-on-one discussion is more appropriate.)

Have volunteers take turns reading excerpts from Scripture or from the commentary. The more each person is involved even in the mundane tasks, the more they'll feel comfortable opening up in more meaningful ways.

The leader should watch the clock and keep the discussion moving. Sometimes there may be more Going Deeper questions than your group can cover in your available time. If you've had a fruitful discussion, it's okay to move on without finishing everything. And if you think the group is getting bogged down on a question or has taken off on a tangent, you can simply say, "Let's go on to question 5." Be sure to save at least ten to fifteen minutes for the Going Forward questions.

Finally, soak your group meetings in prayer—before you begin, during as needed, and always at the end of your time together.

Providence and Faithfulness
(EZRA 1—6)

Before you begin ...
- *Pray for the Holy Spirit to reveal truth and wisdom as you go through this lesson.*
- *Read Ezra 1—6. This lesson references chapters 1 and 2 in* Be Heroic. *It will be helpful for you to have your Bible and a copy of the commentary available as you work through this lesson.*

Getting Started

From the Commentary

More than a century before, the prophet Isaiah had warned the Jews that the people of Judah would be taken captive by Babylon and punished for their sins (Isa. 6:11–12; 10:11–12; 39:5–7), and his prophecy was fulfilled. In 605 BC, Nebuchadnezzar deported the royal family and took the temple vessels to Babylon. In 597, he sent into exile 7,000 "men of might" and 1,000 craftsmen (2 Kings 24:10–16), and in 586, he destroyed Jerusalem and the temple and exiled the rest of the Jews in Babylon, except for "the poor of the land" (2 Kings 25:1–21).

In 538, Cyrus the Great, king of Persia, conqueror of Babylon, issued a decree that permitted the exiled Jews to return to their land and rebuild their temple. This, too, had been prophesied by Isaiah (Isa. 44:28). What Cyrus did twenty-five centuries ago reminds us today of some important spiritual truths.

—*Be Heroic*, page 18

1. Review Ezra 1:1–4. In what ways was God faithful to His word? (See also 1 Kings 8:56; Isa. 44:24–28.) How was He faithful to His covenant? (See also Gen. 12:1–3.) What other truths did Ezra reveal about God's character? Why was this important to the returning Israelites?

More to Consider: Read 2 Chronicles 20:6. In what ways does God "do what He pleases" with the rulers of the earth? (See also Ex. 9:16; Rom. 9:17; Esther; 2 Kings 19:28; Luke 2:1; Acts 12:20–24.)

2. Choose one verse or phrase from Ezra 1—6 that stands out to you. This could be something you're intrigued by, something that makes you uncomfortable, something that puzzles you, something that resonates with you, or just something you want to examine further. Write that here.

Going Deeper

From the Commentary

> God not only stirred the spirit of Cyrus to grant freedom to the captives (Ezra 1:1), but He also stirred the hearts of the Jews to give them the desire to return to Judah (v. 5). "For it is God who works in you both to will and to do for His good pleasure" (Phil. 2:13 NKJV). The same God who ordains the end (the rebuilding of the temple) also ordains the means to the end, in this case, a people willing to go to Judah and work.
>
> Not only did the travelers carry their own personal belongings, but they carried 5,400 gold and silver temple vessels which had been taken from Jerusalem by Nebuchadnezzar (2 Kings 25:8–17; Jer. 52:17–23; Dan. 1:2; 5:1–3). These items were carefully inventoried by the

treasurer and delivered to Sheshbazzar, the appointed ruler of Judah.

Who was Sheshbazzar? He's mentioned four times in Ezra (1:8, 11; 5:14, 16) but not once in any of the other postexilic books. He's called "the prince of Judah" (1:8 KJV, NIV), a title that can mean "leader" or "captain" and often referred to the heads of the tribes of Israel (Num. 1:16, 44; 7:2; Josh. 9:15–21). The word "Judah" in Ezra 1:8 refers to the district of Judah in the Persian Empire, not to the tribe of Judah, so Sheshbazzar was the appointed leader of "the children of the province [of Judah]" (Ezra 2:1).

Many Bible students believe that Sheshbazzar was another name for Zerubbabel, the governor of Judah, who with Joshua the high priest directed the work of the remnant as they rebuilt the city and the temple. He's mentioned twenty times in the postexilic books and, according to 1 Chronicles 3:16–19, was a grandson of King Jehoiakim and therefore a descendant of David.

Ezra 5:16 states that Sheshbazzar laid the foundation of the temple, while Ezra 3:8–13 attributes this to Zerubbabel, and Zechariah 4:9 confirms it. It seems logical to conclude that Sheshbazzar and Zerubbabel were the same person. It wasn't unusual in that day for people to have more than one given name, especially if you were a Jew born in a foreign land.

—*Be Heroic*, pages 21–22

3. Why was it important to keep a careful inventory of the temple treasure? Why does Scripture include such details about the amount of treasure? There's an apparent contradiction in the totals listed in Ezra 1:9–10 compared to 1:11. What is our responsibility as believers when we encounter something that appears to be contradictory in Scripture?

From the Commentary

The long lists of names given in Scripture, including the genealogies, may not be interesting to the average reader, but they're very important to the history of God's people. Unless there's an inheritance involved, most people today are more concerned about the behavior of their descendants than the bloodline of their ancestors, but that wasn't true of the Old Testament Jews. It was necessary for them to be able to prove their ancestry for many reasons.

In Ezra 2:3–20, the names of eighteen Jewish families are listed, totaling 15,604 males. When they took a census, the Jews usually included men twenty years of age and older (Num. 1:1–4), but we aren't certain what procedure was followed here. In Ezra 2:21–35, the volunteers were listed according to twenty-one cities and villages, a total of 8,540 men. We don't know the names of all these 24,144 men, but they were important to the Lord and to the future of the nation and its ministry to the world.

—*Be Heroic*, pages 22–23

4. Review Ezra 2:3–58. Why were genealogies so important to the Jews? How can they help us understand God's covenant with His people? What does this passage reveal to us about God's investment in His people? About how much He values not only the covenant but also each individual person who plays a role in that promise?

From the Commentary

In Ezra 2:59–63, there were 652 people who couldn't prove their Jewish ancestry. (The towns mentioned were in Babylon, not Judah.) Zerubbabel and Joshua didn't send these people back home but allowed them the rights of "strangers and foreigners" (Ex. 22:21, 24; 23:9; Lev. 19:33–34; Deut. 10:18; 14:29).

> We aren't told how many priests were unable to provide adequate credentials, but we are told that they were excluded from serving in the temple.
>
> —*Be Heroic*, page 24

5. Why did God make it clear that any outsider who attempted to serve at the altar would be put to death (Num. 1:51; 3:10)? What does this say about the value He placed on the priesthood? How does that value still apply today to all who are members of the priesthood?

From the Commentary

> Ezra wrote nothing about the long trip (900 miles) or what the Jews experienced during those four difficult months. It reminds us of Moses' description of Abraham and Sarah's journey to Canaan: "and they went forth to go into the land of Canaan; and into the land of Canaan they came" (Gen. 12:5).
>
> —*Be Heroic*, page 25

6. Review Ezra 2:68—3:13. Why didn't Ezra include a record of the Israelites' long trip home? What did Ezra write about instead? Why was this information more important?

From the Commentary

> Following the example of David, when he brought up the ark to Jerusalem (1 Chron. 16), and Solomon, when he dedicated the temple (2 Chron. 7:1–6), the priests and Levites sang praise to the Lord, accompanied by trumpets and cymbals, and the people responded with a great shout that was heard afar off. (See Ps. 47:1; 106:1; 107:1; 118:1–4; 135:3; 136; and 145:1–11.) The people united their hearts and voices in praise to the Lord for His goodness to them.
>
> But at this point, their "togetherness" was interrupted as the young men shouted for joy and the old men wept "with a loud voice."
>
> —*Be Heroic*, page 27

7. Why were the old men weeping in Ezra 3:12? (See also Hag. 2:1–9.) Why might their longing for "the good old days" have been unwelcome? What

role did those good old days play in the destruction of the temple in the first place? What's the difference between longing for the good old days and remembering the past?

From the Commentary

> From the beginning, the remnant faced opposition from the mixed population of the land who really didn't want the Jews inhabiting Jerusalem and rebuilding the temple. Opportunity and opposition usually go together, and the greater the opportunity, the greater the opposition. "For a great and effective door has opened to me," wrote Paul, "and there are many adversaries" (1 Cor. 16:9 NKJV).

> The first attack of the enemy was very subtle: The people of Samaria, the former northern kingdom, offered to work with the Jews to help them build the temple. These people claimed to worship the same God the Jews worshipped, so it seemed logical that they should be allowed to share in the work. On the surface, the Samaritans seemed to be acting like good neighbors, but their offer was insidious and dangerous.

> —*Be Heroic*, page 32

8. What made the Samaritans different from the Jews? (See 2 Kings 17:33; John 4:22.) Why was the Samaritan offer so dangerous? Why was it important during this season in history for the Jewish people to remain culturally "pure"?

More to Consider: It's likely that the Persians wrecked the work the Jews had already completed, and the report that Nehemiah received from his brother described what the Persians had done, not what the Babylonians had done (Neh. 1:1–3). What does this setback (and subsequent rebuilding process) teach us about the resilience of the Jews? About the challenges they would continue to face even upon return from exile? What lessons can the church today take from this little snippet of the Jews' contentious history?

From the Commentary

From 530 to 520 BC, the Jews concentrated on building their own houses and neglected the house of the Lord. The Lord chastened His people to encourage them to obey His commands (Hag. 1:6), but they refused to listen.

—*Be Heroic*, page 35

9. Review Ezra 5:1—6:12. How did God get the work going again after further delays? How did God rely on preachers to encourage the workers? (See 5:1–2.) How did He use local officials? (See 5:3–17.) How did He use Darius the king? (See 6:1–12.)

From the Commentary

> On the twelfth day of the last month of 515 BC, the temple was completed, about seventy years from the destruction of the temple by the Babylonians in 586, and about five and a half years after Haggai and Zechariah called the people back to work (Ezra 5:1–2). God had been faithful to care for His people. He provided encouragement through the preaching of the prophets and even used the authority and wealth of a pagan king to further the work.

> Though there was no ark in the Holy of Holies, and no glory filled the house, the temple was still dedicated to the Lord because it was His house, built for His glory.

> When King Solomon dedicated the temple that he built, he offered so many sacrifices that they couldn't be counted (1 Kings 8:5), plus 142,000 peace offerings which were

shared with the people (1 Kings 8:63). The Jewish remnant offered only 712 sacrifices, but the Lord accepted
them. Most important, they offered twelve male goats as
sin offerings, one for each tribe, because they wanted the
Lord to forgive their sins and give them a new beginning.

Joshua the high priest also consecrated the priests and
Levites for their ministry in the completed temple. David
had organized the priests into twenty-four courses so
they could minister more effectively (1 Chron. 24:1–19).
It wasn't necessary for all of them to serve all the time,
for each course was assigned its week of ministry at the
temple (Luke 1:5, 8). The statement "as it is written in the
book of Moses" (Ezra 6:18) refers to the consecration of
the priests, not their organization. (See Lev. 8—9.)

—*Be Heroic*, pages 38–39

10. Instead of weeping over what they didn't have, the Jews rejoiced over
what they did have. How was this response an act of faith? How did the
Passover celebration solidify their joy in remembering God's promises and
His commitment to keep those promises?

Looking Inward

Take a moment to reflect on all that you've explored thus far in this study of Ezra 1—6. Review your notes and answers and think about how each of these things matters in your life today.

Tips for Small Groups: To get the most out of this section, form pairs or trios and have group members take turns answering these questions. Be honest and as open as you can in this discussion, but most of all, be encouraging and supportive of others. Be sensitive to those who are going through particularly difficult times, and don't press for people to speak if they're uncomfortable doing so.

11. Where have you seen God's faithfulness in your life? Were there times when you doubted His faithfulness? How did that doubt change your relationship with God? How did God use it to bring you closer to Him?

12. What are some ways you long for "the good old days"? What are the benefits of looking back? What are the dangers? How can you celebrate the goodness of today without dishonoring the goodness of yesterday?

13. What promises from God do you consider most important? How do you rely on God's promises in your daily life? How do you respond when God's promises appear to be "delayed"?

Going Forward

14. Think of one or two things that you have learned that you'd like to work on in the coming week. Remember that this is all about quality, not quantity. It's better to work on one specific area of life and do it well than to work on many and do poorly (or to be so overwhelmed that you simply don't try).

Do you want to trust one of God's promises? Be specific. Go back through Ezra 1—6 and put a star next to the phrase or verse that is most encouraging to you. Consider memorizing this verse.

Real-Life Application Ideas: The Jews finally made their way back to Jerusalem after a long exile. But life wasn't easy once they'd returned. The building process was long and fraught with challenges. This week, consider the "building projects" you have in your life. Perhaps they're work related or family related. Maybe they're actual physical projects, or maybe they're spiritual. Rededicate yourself to doing the hard work, and look for ways to shore up support for the inevitable challenges ahead. You might want to create a support group for your building project—people who can help encourage you when things get tough. Then forge ahead with confidence, listening for God's wisdom in the process.

Seeking Help

15. Write a prayer below (or simply pray one in silence), inviting God to work on your mind and heart in those areas you've noted in the Going Forward section. Be honest about your desires and fears.

Notes for Small Groups:

- *Look for ways to put into practice the things you wrote in the Going Forward section. Talk with other group members about your ideas and commit to being accountable to one another.*

- *During the coming week, ask the Holy Spirit to continue to reveal truth to you from what you've read and studied.*

- *Before you start the next lesson, read Ezra 7—10. For more in-depth lesson preparation, read chapters 3 and 4, "The Good Hand of God" and "The Grace of God," in* Be Heroic.

God's Grace
(EZRA 7—10)

Before you begin …
- *Pray for the Holy Spirit to reveal truth and wisdom as you go through this lesson.*
- *Read Ezra 7—10. This lesson references chapters 3 and 4 in* Be Heroic. *It will be helpful for you to have your Bible and a copy of the commentary available as you work through this lesson.*

Getting Started

From the Commentary

When talk show hosts and hostesses ask successful people the secret of their great achievements, the answers they get are varied and sometimes contradictory. Some successful people will give credit to their sobriety and personal discipline, while others will boast that they lived just the way they pleased whether anybody liked it or not. "I always maintain my integrity" is counterbalanced by "I pushed my way to the top no matter who got stepped on."

But if we had interviewed Ezra and asked him the secret of his successful life, he would have said humbly, "The good hand of the Lord was upon me."

That God's good hand was upon this man doesn't minimize the importance of his personal piety or his great ability as a scholar, nor does it ignore the great help King Artaxerxes gave him.

—*Be Heroic*, page 43

1. Why does the book of Ezra repeat the phrase "the hand of the Lord was on me/him/us" so many times in chapters 7 and 8? Underline all six occurrences. What do these tell us about the kind of people God uses to accomplish His will? (See also John 15:5.)

2. Choose one verse or phrase from Ezra 7—10 that stands out to you. This could be something you're intrigued by, something that makes you uncomfortable, something that puzzles you, something that resonates with you, or just something you want to examine further. Write that here.

Going Deeper

From the Commentary

It was the year 458 BC, and Artaxerxes I was King of Persia (465–424). Nearly sixty years had passed since the completion of the temple in Jerusalem, and the Jewish remnant was having a very difficult time. It was then that God raised up Ezra to lead a second group of refugees from Babylon to Judah to bring financial and spiritual support to the work and to help rebuild the city.

Every person is important to God and God's work, but, as Dr. Lee Roberson has often said, "Everything rises and falls with leadership." When God wanted to deliver Israel from Egypt, He raised up Moses and Aaron. When Israel was divided and defeated, He called Samuel to teach the Word and David to serve as king. Richard Nixon was right when he said that leaders are people who "make a difference," and Ezra was that kind of man.

—Be Heroic, page 44

3. How does God use inferior leaders to judge a nation? (See Isa. 3:1–8.) What made Ezra a superior leader? How does this show God's blessing on a nation?

More to Consider: Some priests in the Jewish remnant couldn't prove their ancestry (Ezra 2:61–63), but Ezra wasn't among them. He had the best of credentials and could prove his lineage all the way back to Aaron, the first high priest. Read Deuteronomy 4:40 and Psalm 128. What does God promise about the descendants of the godly?

From the Commentary

When you recall that Ezra was born in Babylon, you can better appreciate his achievement as a skilled student of the Jewish Scriptures. Undoubtedly, some of the priests had brought copies of the Old Testament scrolls with them to Babylon, and these became very precious to the exiled spiritual leaders of the nation. There was no Jewish temple in Babylon, so the priests and Levites weren't obligated to minister, but some of them, like Ezra, devoted themselves to the study and teaching of the Word of God.

—*Be Heroic*, page 45

4. In what ways did Ezra represent a good student of God's Word? (See Ezra 7:10.) How was his way of approaching God's Word similar to what the psalmist described in Psalm 119:97? How did the king recognize and affirm Ezra's great knowledge of the Scriptures? (See Ezra 7:11–26.)

From the Commentary

Just as God had worked in the heart and mind of Cyrus (Ezra 1:1–4) and Darius (6:1–12), so He moved upon Artaxerxes I to permit Ezra and his people to return to their land. After hearing Ezra's requests, Artaxerxes took several steps to assist the Jews in this important undertaking.

Authorization (Ezra 7:11–12, 25–26). First, Artaxerxes appointed Ezra as the leader of the group and also as the king's agent in Judah, even to the extent of giving him the right to inflict capital punishment on offenders (v. 26). From the way the king described Ezra in his official letter, it's clear that he was impressed with this Jewish priest-scribe and the law which was the center of his life and ministry.

Liberation (Ezra 7:13–14). In his official letter, Artaxerxes gave the Jews the privilege to leave Babylon and go to Jerusalem with Ezra and join the remnant in rebuilding the city walls (4:12). Refer back to Ezra 4:7–23 for the account of the trials the Jews had in spite of the king's encouragement, and keep in mind that it was the rebuilding of the city, not the temple, that was involved, along with the spiritual restoration of the people.

Compensation (Ezra 7:15–26). The Lord had told the struggling people in Jerusalem, "The silver is Mine, and the gold is Mine" (Hag. 2:8 NKJV), and now He proved it by opening the royal treasury and providing money to buy sacrifices to be offered at the temple in Jerusalem. The king commanded his officers beyond the river to give the Jews money out of the local royal treasury and defined the limits (Ezra 7:22). A hundred talents of silver would be nearly four tons of silver!

—Be Heroic, pages 47–48

5. Review Ezra 7:11–28. How do we know that what Artaxerxes did for the Jews was because of the good hand of God? Why was Artaxerxes concerned that the temple ministry be strong and steady? What were his motives? What's the significance of the narrative turning to first person ("I" instead of "you") in verses 27–28? What is Ezra's message in these verses?

From the Commentary

As these Jewish émigrés trudged through the wilderness, I wonder if they sang Psalm 121 to each other?

They left Babylon on the first day of the first month (Ezra 7:9), tarried three days at the Ahava canal (8:15), and then left that encampment on the twelfth day of the first month (8:31), arriving at Jerusalem on the first day of the fifth month (7:9). They covered at least 900 miles in four months' time, and the good hand of God protected them and their possessions all the way.

—*Be Heroic*, pages 51–52

6. Review Ezra 8:31–36. How did God protect the travelers in their journey? What role did rest play in the journey? What role did worship play? What does this tell us about rest and worship in today's church?

From the Commentary

Ezra must have experienced great joy and satisfaction when he found himself in the Holy City, worshipping at the restored temple and ministering to the spiritual needs of the people. He certainly would have had an easier life had he remained "Scholar in Residence" for the exiles in Babylon, but an easier life wasn't on Ezra's agenda. God had called him to serve the Jewish remnant and teach them the law of God, and he was obedient to God's call.

But four months after his arrival (Ezra 7:9; 10:9), he learned that all wasn't well in Jerusalem because over one hundred civil and religious leaders of the nation were guilty of deliberately disobeying the law that Ezra had come to teach.

—*Be Heroic*, page 57

7. In what ways were the people disobeying what Ezra had come to teach? How did Ezra face this problem of disobedience? What message does his response give us for dealing with disobedience in the body of Christ today?

From the Commentary

How privileged the remnant was to have a spiritual leader like Ezra! He had been given special authority by the king (Ezra 7:25–26), so you can see how serious it was for him to know what these men had done. Depending on the offense, Ezra could banish people from the community, confiscate their wealth, or even order their execution! But Ezra was first of all a man of God who sought God's best for his people, and he identified with them and made their burdens his burdens. He was supremely a man of prayer.

—*Be Heroic*, page 59

8. What was Ezra's initial response to the people's sins (Ezra 9:3)? How did he confront them? Why did he go to the temple first? In what ways did he express his sorrow? How did the people respond to his actions?

More to Consider: One of the maladies of society today is that people are no longer shocked by sin and willing to do something about it. Political leaders can flagrantly break the law and not only get away with it but also be admired by the public and be elected to office again. Why might polls indicate that "character" isn't an important factor when it comes to choosing leaders? What does that say about our society? How does Matthew 5:13–16 speak to this concern?

From the Commentary

Like both Nehemiah (Neh. 1:4–10) and Daniel (Dan. 9), Ezra identified himself with the people and their sins and spoke to God about "our iniquities" and not "their iniquities." Israel was one covenant nation before God, and the sins of one person affected all the people. For example, when Achan disobeyed God at Jericho, God said to Joshua, *"Israel* has sinned" (Josh. 7:11 NKJV, italics mine). The same principle applies to the local church (1 Cor. 5:6–8). Unless sin is dealt with, the whole assembly becomes defiled.

Like the publican in our Lord's parable (Luke 18:9–14), Ezra was too ashamed to look up to heaven as he prayed. The inability to blush because of sin is a mark of hypocrisy and superficial spiritual experience (Jer. 6:13–15). "Are they ashamed of their loathsome conduct? No, they have no shame at all; they do not even know how to blush" (Jer. 8:12 NIV). Words and actions that would have made earlier generations blush in shame are today part of the normal entertainment diet of the average TV viewer. When a nation turns sin into entertainment and laughs at what ought to make us weep, we are in desperate need of revival.

—Be Heroic, page 61

9. Why was Ezra so ashamed of the people (Ezra 9:7)? Why is it so important that Ezra included himself in the discussion of their sins and iniquities? What lesson does this give us for today's leaders?

From the Commentary

Never underestimate the power of the prayers of one dedicated believer (James 5:16–18), for the intercession of only one concerned person can make a difference in what God will do to and for His people. As Ezra prayed and wept at the altar before the house of God, "a very great congregation of men and women and children" came together, and they fell under conviction of sin.

As I watch the contemporary religious scene, I note that churches occasionally feature "Christian comedians" and "Christian clowns," but not much is said about people who know how to weep and pray. As much as anyone else, I appreciate a sense of humor and a good laugh, but there comes a time when God's people need to stop laughing and start weeping and confessing. "Lament and mourn and weep! Let your laughter be turned to mourning and your joy to gloom. Humble yourselves in the sight of the Lord, and He will lift you up" (James 4:9–10 NKJV). That's God's formula for revival.

—Be Heroic, pages 64–65

10. Review Ezra 10:1–8. Why is lamenting such a lost "art" in today's church? How did Ezra model a healthy way to mourn? How can mourning be turned to celebrating?

Looking Inward

Take a moment to reflect on all that you've explored thus far in this study of Ezra 7—10. Review your notes and answers and think about how each of these things matters in your life today.

Tips for Small Groups: To get the most out of this section, form pairs or trios and have group members take turns answering these questions. Be honest and as open as you can in this discussion, but most of all, be encouraging and supportive of others. Be sensitive to those who are going through particularly difficult times, and don't press for people to speak if they're uncomfortable doing so.

11. In what ways are you a dedicated student of God's Word? How do you approach the Bible in practical ways? How can a dedication to regular study help you grow your personal faith?

12. What role does rest play in your faith story? How does rest help you grow in faith? How does it help you worship? What happens when you don't rest enough?

13. Do you practice lamenting or mourning? How does that affect your spiritual life? Your worship? What makes it difficult to mourn or lament? Why is it important?

Going Forward

14. Think of one or two things that you have learned that you'd like to work on in the coming week. Remember that this is all about quality, not quantity. It's better to work on one specific area of life and do it well than to work on many and do poorly (or to be so overwhelmed that you simply don't try).

Is there a sin you want to lament and turn away from? Be specific. Go back through Ezra 7—10 and put a star next to the phrase or verse that is most encouraging to you. Consider memorizing this verse.

Real-Life Application Ideas: Help to organize a small worship time for people to lament and mourn the things they have lost. This could be something just for you and family members or small-group members. Or maybe you can coordinate a church-wide service. Make this time a quiet, solemn experience—allowing people to express their tears, both literally and figuratively. Then close the service in a reverent time of worship, thanking God for using all our tears to bring us closer to Him. Begin incorporating regular times for mourning and lamenting in your personal worship as well.

Seeking Help

15. Write a prayer below (or simply pray one in silence), inviting God to work on your mind and heart in those areas you've noted in the Going Forward section. Be honest about your desires and fears.

Notes for Small Groups:

- *Look for ways to put into practice the things you wrote in the Going Forward section. Talk with other group members about your ideas and commit to being accountable to one another.*
- *During the coming week, ask the Holy Spirit to continue to reveal truth to you from what you've read and studied.*
- *Before you start the next lesson, read Haggai 1. For more in-depth lesson preparation, read chapter 5, "Stirring Up God's People," in* Be Heroic.

Stirring Things Up

(HAGGAI 1)

Before you begin …
- *Pray for the Holy Spirit to reveal truth and wisdom as you go through this lesson.*
- *Read Haggai 1. This lesson references chapter 5 in* Be Heroic. *It will be helpful for you to have your Bible and a copy of the commentary available as you work through this lesson.*

Getting Started

From the Commentary

While their names aren't in the official lists, the Prophets Haggai and Zechariah were probably among the nearly 50,000 Jewish exiles who left Babylon for Judah in 537 BC, encouraged by the edict of King Cyrus (Ezra 1:1–4; 5:1–2; 6:14). Haggai 2:3 suggests that Haggai had seen Solomon's temple before it was destroyed and therefore was an old man, while Zechariah is called a young man (Zech. 2:4). These two prophets belonged to different generations, but this didn't hinder them from working together to get the temple rebuilt.

We know nothing about Haggai's family background, call, or personal life. When the work on the temple had been stopped for sixteen years (536–520), Haggai and Zechariah suddenly began to preach and to encourage the people to put God first and get back to work (Hag. 1:1; Zech. 1:1).

—*Be Heroic*, page 71

1. What was Haggai's primary message in Haggai 1:2–11? How did he remind the people of the covenant promises recorded in Deuteronomy 28?

2. Choose one verse or phrase from Haggai 1 that stands out to you. This could be something you're intrigued by, something that makes you uncomfortable, something that puzzles you, something that resonates with you, or just something you want to examine further. Write that here.

Going Deeper

From the Commentary

> When the foundations of the temple were laid in Jerusalem in the year 536 BC, the younger men shouted for joy while the older men wept (Ezra 3:8–13). Although Haggai probably had seen Solomon's temple in its glory (Hag. 2:3), he was undoubtedly among those who expressed joy, for the Lord was at work among His people.
>
> But it doesn't take long for zeal to cool and God's people to grow apathetic, especially when opposition began an ominous growl that soon became a roar. The shout awakened the enemies of the Jews, aroused official opposition, and caused the work to stop (Ezra 4:1–6, 24). The temple lay unfinished from 536 to 520, when Haggai and Zechariah brought God's message to Zerubbabel and Joshua.
>
> —*Be Heroic*, page 73

3. Why was it important that the people finish building the temple? What did it reveal to the people about God's character? About God's priorities? About the people's priorities?

From the Commentary

The first statement in the divine message (Hag. 1:1–4) went right to the heart of the problem and exposed the hypocrisy and unbelief of the people.

"It isn't time to rebuild the house of the Lord" was their defense of their inactivity. Billy Sunday called an excuse "the skin of a reason stuffed with a lie," and Benjamin Franklin wrote, "I never knew a man who was good at making excuses who was good at anything else."

The first congregation I pastored met in a corrugated metal tabernacle that should have been replaced years before, but whenever somebody would suggest a building program, some of the fearful people would resurrect their excuses for maintaining the status quo. "The economy isn't good, and there might be another strike," was the major excuse we heard, but in that part of the country, there were always strikes! And who can predict or control the economy? "Our pastors don't stay long," one member told me, "and it would be a tragedy to be in a building program without a leader." But the Lord led us to build a lovely sanctuary, and He saw us through!

What more evidence did the Jewish people need that God's time had come? How could they doubt that it was God's will for them to rebuild the temple and restore true worship in Jerusalem? Hadn't God moved King Cyrus to free the exiles and commission them to return to Jerusalem for that very purpose? (See 2 Chron. 36:22–23;

Ezra 1:1–4.) Didn't the king generously give them the money and materials they needed, and didn't the Lord graciously protect the exiles carrying the temple treasures as they traveled from Babylon to Judah?

—*Be Heroic*, pages 73–74

4. Why did the people keep giving excuses for their inactivity? On what basis did they refuse to build? What excuses do people who refuse to obey God and build His house give today?

More to Consider: The people were terribly inconsistent—it wasn't time to build the house of God, but it was time to build their own houses! And some of the people had built not just ordinary dwellings but "paneled houses," the kind that kings built for themselves (1 Kings 7:3, 7; Jer. 22:14). Read Matthew 6:33. How does this verse apply to the people's actions (or lack of action)? How does this principle still apply today?

From Today's World

Depending on whom you ask, the church is either in crisis or ripe for revival. Certainly both can be true at the same time, since there are plenty of examples throughout history of church failings and church growth occurring simultaneously. One of the biggest challenges the local church faces is prioritizing. Like the Jews upon return from exile, the people of the church have to decide what's most important to work on right now. Is it the church infrastructure? The programs? Outreach? Worship? Or is it individual spiritual growth? There is no shortage of things to address, and the success or failure of any church is often determined by what gets the highest priority.

5. What should today's church focus on above all else? What does that look like in the local church? What leads to messed-up priorities in a church? How do priorities define a church's culture? Its chances for continued growth?

From the Commentary

Haggai's second admonition (1:5–6, 9–11) invited the people to examine their lifestyle and actions in the light of the covenant God made with them before the nation entered the land of Canaan (Lev. 26; Deut. 27—28). The word translated "consider" in the KJV is translated "give careful thought to" in the NIV (Hag. 1:5). It was time for the people to do some serious self-examination before the Lord.

God's covenant stated clearly that He would bless them if they obeyed His law and discipline them if they disobeyed. "If you do not obey Me, then I will punish you seven times more for your sins. I will break the pride of your power; I will make your heavens like iron and your earth like bronze. And your strength shall be spent in vain; for your land shall not yield its produce, nor shall the trees of the land yield their fruit" (Lev. 26:18–20 NKJV; see Deut. 28:38–40).

—*Be Heroic*, page 76

6. In what ways did the people sow abundantly but reap a meager harvest? How was their strength spent in vain? How does this continue to happen in today's church? How do we confront this tendency?

From the Commentary

> Because the Jews returned to the land in obedience to the
> Lord, they thought He would give them special blessings
> because of their sacrifices, but they were disappointed
> (Hag. 1:9). Instead, the Lord called for a drought and
> withheld both the dew and the rain. He took His blessing
> away from the men who labored in the fields, vineyards,
> and orchards. In verse 11, Haggai named the basic prod-
> ucts that the people needed to survive: water, grain, wine,
> and oil (Deut. 7:13; 11:14).
>
> —*Be Heroic*, page 77

7. What did the prophet reveal as the reason for the people's continued
struggle (Hag. 1:9)? In what ways is this similar to Matthew 6:33? How
would things have been different if the people had believed what God had
promised in His covenants?

From the Commentary

When the Babylonian army set fire to the temple, this destroyed the great timbers that helped to hold the massive stonework together. The stones were still usable, but the interior woodwork had been demolished and burned and had to be replaced.

According to Ezra 3:7, the Jews purchased wood from Tyre and Sidon, just as Solomon had done when he built the original temple (1 Kings 5:6–12). Now Haggai commanded the men to go into the forests on the mountains and cut down timber to be used for repairing and rebuilding the temple. What happened to that original supply of wood? Did the people use it for themselves? Did some clever entrepreneur profit by selling wood that had been bought with the king's grant? We don't know, but we wonder where the people got the wood for their paneled houses when no wood was available for God's house.

—*Be Heroic*, page 78

8. Review Haggai 1:7–8. Why did the people have to replace inferior materials? Why is it common for people to purchase the best for themselves and give to the Lord whatever is left over? (See Mal. 1:6–8.) How do we commit a sin when we give God our second best?

More to Consider: "Hallowed be your name" is the first petition in the Lord's Prayer (Matt. 6:9), but it's often the last thing we think about as we seek to serve God. Read John 8:28–29 and Matthew 5:16. How do these verses provide us a good example to follow in honoring God?

From the Commentary

When God speaks to us by His Word, there's only one acceptable response, and that's obedience. We don't weigh the options, we don't examine the alternatives, and we don't negotiate the terms. We simply do what God tells us to do and leave the rest with Him. "Faith is not believing in spite of evidence," said the British preacher Geoffrey Studdert-Kennedy; "it's obeying in spite of consequence."

—*Be Heroic*, page 79

9. Review Haggai 1:12–15. What motivated the people to obedience? How does obedience lead to further truth? (See John 7:17.)

From the Commentary

Haggai delivered this first message on August 29, 520 BC, but it wasn't until September 21 that the people resumed their work on the temple. Why the three-week delay? For one thing, it was the month when figs and grapes were harvested, and the people didn't want to lose their crop. Also, before they could build, the Jews had to remove the debris from the temple site, take inventory of their supplies, and organize their work crews. It would have been foolish to rush ahead totally unprepared. It's also possible that they took time to confess their sins and purify themselves so that their work would be pleasing to the Lord (Ps. 51:16–19).

—*Be Heroic*, page 80

10. What lessons can the church today learn from the Jewish remnant of Haggai's day? How can we exchange excuses for action? How can we embrace humility over hubris?

Looking Inward

Take a moment to reflect on all that you've explored thus far in this study of Haggai 1. Review your notes and answers and think about how each of these things matters in your life today.

Tips for Small Groups: To get the most out of this section, form pairs or trios and have group members take turns answering these questions. Be honest and as open as you can in this discussion, but most of all, be encouraging and supportive of others. Be sensitive to those who are going through particularly difficult times, and don't press for people to speak if they're uncomfortable doing so.

11. Describe a time when you offered up excuses instead of doing what you knew God wanted you to do. Why did you avoid what you knew was right? How do those excuses look to you now? What did you learn through that experience?

12. How do you prioritize your life? What role does God play in setting those priorities? Do your priorities change over time? What is your top priority in your relationship with God? With others?

13. Some of the returning exiles gave their second best to God and took the best for themselves. Have you ever been tempted to do this? Explain. Why is it so difficult to give your best to God? What role does trust play in this decision?

Going Forward

14. Think of one or two things that you have learned that you'd like to work on in the coming week. Remember that this is all about quality, not quantity. It's better to work on one specific area of life and do it well than to work on many and do poorly (or to be so overwhelmed that you simply don't try).

Do you want to examine your priorities and make changes if necessary? Be specific. Go back through Haggai 1 and put a star next to the phrase or verse that is most encouraging to you. Consider memorizing this verse.

Real-Life Application Ideas: This week, take some time to consider whether you're giving God your best or your leftovers. Take a look at not only the way you use your money but also the way you organize your time and your thoughts. If you find that you're giving less than your best, make a plan to change that.

Seeking Help

15. Write a prayer below (or simply pray one in silence), inviting God to work on your mind and heart in those areas you've noted in the Going Forward section. Be honest about your desires and fears.

Notes for Small Groups:
- *Look for ways to put into practice the things you wrote in the Going Forward section. Talk with other group members about your ideas and commit to being accountable to one another.*
- *During the coming week, ask the Holy Spirit to continue to reveal truth to you from what you've read and studied.*
- *Before you start the next lesson, read Haggai 2. For more in-depth lesson preparation, read chapter 6, "Keeping the Work Alive," in* Be Heroic.

The Work
(HAGGAI 2)

Before you begin …
- *Pray for the Holy Spirit to reveal truth and wisdom as you go through this lesson.*
- *Read Haggai 2. This lesson references chapter 6 in* Be Heroic. *It will be helpful for you to have your Bible and a copy of the commentary available as you work through this lesson.*

Getting Started

From the Commentary

It's one thing to get God's people back to work and quite another thing to keep them on the job. Dr. Bob Jones Sr. often said that the greatest ability a person can possess is dependability, but too often potential workers excuse themselves and say, "Here am I, Lord; send somebody else." "To work is to pray," said Saint Augustine, and God's people can do any legitimate task to the glory of God (1 Cor. 10:31).

—*Be Heroic*, page 83

1. Why was rebuilding the temple so important to the returning exiles? What symbolic purpose did it play in their faith story? How was the temple a testimony to the unbelieving nations?

2. Choose one verse or phrase from Haggai 2 that stands out to you. This could be something you're intrigued by, something that makes you uncomfortable, something that puzzles you, something that resonates with you, or just something you want to examine further. Write that here.

Going Deeper

From the Commentary

When the foundation of the temple had been laid sixteen years before, some of the older men had looked back in sorrow as they remembered the glory and beauty of

Solomon's temple (Ezra 3:8–13). It's likely that Haggai was a member of the older generation and had seen the temple before it was destroyed, but he certainly didn't weep with the rest of his peers. He rejoiced that the work had begun, and he wanted to see it completed.

Rather than ignore the problem of discouragement that was sure to come when the people contrasted the two temples, the prophet faced the problem head-on. He picked an important day on which to deliver his message: October 17, the last day of the Feast of Tabernacles. This feast was devoted to praising God for the harvest and for remembering Israel's pilgrim days in the wilderness (Lev. 23:34–43).

—*Be Heroic*, pages 83–84

3. Review Haggai 2:1–3. Why was it appropriate to dedicate the rebuilt temple at the Feast of Tabernacles? Why was it also meaningful to dedicate it at the same time of year when the first temple, which Solomon built, had been dedicated (1 Kings 8:1–2)? The restored building had nothing of the splendor of Solomon's temple, but it was still God's house. How were the people supposed to feel about that? How can we apply the wisdom gained from this event to the church today?

More to Consider: During the Feast of Tabernacles, the Jews had the book of Deuteronomy read to them (Deut. 31:9–13). What do you think the purpose of this was? Read Joshua 1:6–7, 9 and 1 Chronicles 22:13; 28:10, 20. What is the common theme in these passages? What does it mean to "be strong"?

From the Commentary

The promise of God's presence with His people is guaranteed by His unchanging Word (Hag. 2:5). When the tabernacle was dedicated by Moses, God's presence moved in (Ex. 40:34–38), for the Lord had promised to dwell with His people. "Then I will dwell among the Israelites and be their God. They will know that I am the LORD their God, who brought them out of Egypt so that I might dwell among them" (Ex. 29:45–46 NIV). The same Holy Spirit who enabled Moses and the elders to lead the people (Num. 11:16–17, 25; Isa. 63:11) would enable the Jews to finish building the temple.

—*Be Heroic*, page 85

4. How is God's presence represented in the Old Testament? How does that compare to God's presence after the coming of the Holy Spirit? Why was it important to trust God's presence in Haggai's time? How did that play out in the tabernacle's dedication?

From Today's World

While some churches struggle to pay their heating bills, others are building bigger and better buildings to handle a growing membership. This has been true as long as there have been churches, but today, the rise of megachurches has made the divide between the shrinking churches and the growing churches even wider. Another thing that hasn't changed over the years is the controversy that often accompanies a building program.

5. Why are building programs such a contentious thing for churches? How is today's church building like and unlike the temple of Haggai's time? What are some lessons we can apply to today's building programs from how the Jews approached the rebuilding of the temple? What are some things we shouldn't apply?

From the Commentary

God not only promised the coming of Messiah and the glory of God in the future temples, but He also promised peace (Hag. 2:9). "In this place" refers to the city of Jerusalem where the Messiah will reign as "Prince of Peace" (Isa. 9:6). Those who believe on Jesus today have peace with God (Rom. 5:1) because of His atoning death

and victorious resurrection (Col. 1:20; John 20:19–21).
They may also enjoy the "peace of God" as they yield to
Christ and trust wholly in Him (Phil. 4:6–9).

—*Be Heroic*, page 87

6. What promises did the remnant have of provision from the government?
(See Ezra 1:4; 3:7; 6:4.) To what extent were these promises kept? How
do these promises line up with God's promises to take care of the people?
How can we know which promises are from God and which are from
humankind? What did trusting God to provide look like to the people in
Haggai's time? What does that look like today?

From the Commentary

About two months later (Dec. 18), the Lord spoke to
Haggai again and gave him a message about sin. God
couldn't bless the people the way He wanted to because
they were defiled, so it was important that they keep
themselves clean before the Lord.

Haggai went to the priests, who were the authorities on
this subject, and asked them two simple questions, not for

his own education (he certainly knew the law) but for the benefit of the people who were present.

Question #1—holiness (Hag. 2:11–12). When an animal was presented on the altar as a sacrifice, the meat was considered holy; that is, it belonged to the Lord and was set apart to be used only as He instructed. The priests and their families were permitted to eat portions of some of the sacrifices, but they had to be careful how they ate it, where they ate it, and what they did with the leftovers (Lev. 6:8—7:38).

"If a garment containing a piece of consecrated meat touches food," Haggai asked, "does the garment make the food holy?" The priests replied, "No." Why? Because you can't transmit holiness in such a simple manner. Even though the garment is holy (set apart) because of the sanctified meat, this holiness can't be imparted to other objects by the garment.

Question #2—defilement (Hag. 2:13). "Suppose somebody touched a dead body and became unclean," Haggai said. "Could that person touch another person and make him unclean?" The answer was obviously yes. Haggai had made his point: You can transmit defilement from one thing or person to another, but you can't transmit sanctity. The same principle applies in the area of health: You can transmit your sickness to healthy people and make them sick, but you can't share your health with them.

—*Be Heroic*, pages 87–88

7. Why were "clean" and "unclean" such important concepts to the Jews living under the old covenant? (See Lev. 14.) Why did they have such specific rules about what defined "clean" and "unclean"? How did those rules help preserve the integrity of the temple? How did those rules later become an obstacle for believers?

From the Commentary

Haggai was issuing a call to repentance, and with that call came the assurance of God's blessing (Hag. 2:18–19). He was reminding the people of the promise God gave Solomon after the dedication of the temple: "If my people, which are called by my name, shall humble themselves, and pray, and seek my face, and turn from their wicked ways; then will I hear from heaven, and will forgive their sin, and will heal their land" (2 Chron. 7:14).

Had the workers been devoted to the Lord when the foundation of the temple was laid, God's blessing would have followed immediately, but the people were sinful at heart, and their sin grieved the Lord and defiled their work. "Is the seed yet in the barn?" he asked his congregation (Hag. 2:19), and they would have had to answer, "No." It was

late December and the men had just plowed the fields
for the winter crops. Haggai was calling on them to trust
God for the future harvest.

—Be Heroic, page 89

8. How are Haggai's words in 2:19 another example of Matthew 6:33?
Many local church constitutions assign to the elders the spiritual direction
of the church and to the deacons the responsibilities for the material aspects
of the ministry. What are the challenges and risks of dividing the tasks like
this? How can we show our spiritual devotion to God through the way we
treat material things?

More to Consider: Read Proverbs 14:34. How does this verse define
the core cause of all the "challenges" God's people faced, including the
rebuilding of the temple? Why did Haggai ask the people to look back
and then to look within? What would they find?

From the Commentary

Haggai has encouraged the Jewish people to stay on the job and finish God's house. Now he has a special word of encouragement for Zerubbabel the governor, and it was delivered on the same day as the third message, December 18. Being a faithful preacher of the Word, Haggai was always listening for God's voice and sensitive to whatever the Lord wanted him to say and do.

Zerubbabel was the grandson of King Jehoiachin (Jeconiah, Matt. 1:12; Coniah, Jer. 22:24, 28) and therefore of the royal line of David. But instead of wearing a crown and sitting on a throne, Zerubbabel was the humble governor of a struggling remnant of the Jewish nation, trying to complete the building of a rather inglorious temple. What a discouraging situation for a royal prince to be in!

So, God gave His servant Haggai a special word of encouragement for the governor. Were the nations around Jerusalem larger and stronger? Rest assured that the Lord will care for His people Israel as He has always done in the past. The same God who enabled Moses to defeat Egypt, and Joshua to conquer the nations in Canaan, would protect His people so that His purposes could be fulfilled through them. Israel will endure until the last days, and then the Lord will defeat her enemies and establish her in her kingdom.

The Lord called Zerubbabel "my servant," an exclusive title reserved for specially chosen people, and Zerubbabel was indeed chosen by the Lord. God compared him to a royal signet ring. The signet ring was used by kings to put their official "signature" on documents (Est. 3:10; 8:8, 10), the guarantee that the king would keep his promise and fulfill the terms of the document.

Zerubbabel's ancestor, King Jehoiachin (Coniah), had been rejected by God, but Zerubbabel was accepted by God. "'As I live,' says the LORD, 'though Coniah the son of Jehoiakim, king of Judah, were the signet on My right hand, yet I would pluck you off'" (Jer. 22:24 NKJV). God was reversing the judgment and renewing His promise that the Davidic line would not die out but would one day give the world a Savior. That's why we find Zerubbabel named in the genealogies of Jesus Christ (Matt. 1:12; Luke 3:27).

—Be Heroic, pages 90–91

9. How would this message have encouraged Zerubbabel? What does it mean to be called by God for a special work? How can knowing that God sees each of us as uniquely qualified affect the way we pursue His kingdom work?

From the Commentary

We can't leave Haggai without noting some practical lessons for God's people today.

1. The work of God is begun, sustained, and encouraged by the Word of God.

2. God's servants must work together to build God's temple.

3. When the outlook is bleak, try the uplook.

4. Putting God first is the guarantee of God's best blessing.

5. Apart from the power of the Holy Spirit, our labors are in vain.

—*Be Heroic*, pages 92–93

10. Review each of the five themes listed in the commentary excerpt. How did each of these apply to Haggai's situation? How do they apply to the body of Christ today? What does each of these look like in everyday, practical terms?

Looking Inward

Take a moment to reflect on all that you've explored thus far in this study of Haggai 2. Review your notes and answers and think about how each of these things matters in your life today.

Tips for Small Groups: To get the most out of this section, form pairs or trios and have group members take turns answering these questions. Be honest and as open as you can in this discussion, but most of all, be encouraging and supportive of others. Be sensitive to those who are going through particularly difficult times, and don't press for people to speak if they're uncomfortable doing so.

11. Think of a challenge you recently faced. Where did you find your strength to face that challenge? If you struggled to find that strength, what could you have done to be more confident? What does it look like to you to count on the Holy Spirit for strength? Is that easy for you? Explain.

12. God's promises are many, though they may not always seem specific to your current circumstance. Where do you turn to find God's promises? How do you apply them to your own life? What are the promises you have a hard time accepting or believing?

13. In the Old Testament world, cleanness was a requirement for all who might approach God in the temple. But today, Jesus invites us to come to Him just as we are. Do you ever hesitate to reach out to God when you feel "unclean"? Why? Why do you think you need to look a certain way or act a certain way to stand before God? What does it mean to you that Jesus has cleared a path so you can stand before Him no matter what your story is?

Going Forward

14. Think of one or two things that you have learned that you'd like to work on in the coming week. Remember that this is all about quality, not quantity. It's better to work on one specific area of life and do it well than to work on many and do poorly (or to be so overwhelmed that you simply don't try).

Do you want to rely on the strength of the Holy Spirit in a difficult circumstance? Be specific. Go back through Haggai 2 and put a star next to the phrase or verse that is most encouraging to you. Consider memorizing this verse.

Real-Life Application Ideas: God called Zerubbabel to do a very special work during the rebuilding of the temple. What is God's call on your life today? Are there some things you and you alone can do to advance God's kingdom? Invite friends and leaders and others to share what they think your special gifts might be. Then spend time in prayer and study, asking God to reveal your unique role in the church for this season of your life. (It could change tomorrow—God does move in mysterious ways after all.) Then pursue that work with confidence, trusting the strength of the Holy Spirit to guide you.

Seeking Help

15. Write a prayer below (or simply pray one in silence), inviting God to work on your mind and heart in those areas you've noted in the Going Forward section. Be honest about your desires and fears.

Notes for Small Groups:

- *Look for ways to put into practice the things you wrote in the Going Forward section. Talk with other group members about your ideas and commit to being accountable to one another.*

- *During the coming week, ask the Holy Spirit to continue to reveal truth to you from what you've read and studied.*

- *Before you start the next lesson, read Zechariah 1—2. For more in-depth lesson preparation, read chapter 7, "God and His People," in* Be Heroic.

God and His People
(ZECHARIAH 1—2)

Before you begin ...
- *Pray for the Holy Spirit to reveal truth and wisdom as you go through this lesson.*
- *Read Zechariah 1—2. This lesson references chapter 7 in* Be Heroic. *It will be helpful for you to have your Bible and a copy of the commentary available as you work through this lesson.*

Getting Started

From the Commentary

Thirty-one men in the Bible have the name Zechariah, which means "the Lord remembers." (See Zech. 10:9 and Luke 1:72.) The prophet Zechariah was a young man when he wrote this book (Zech. 2:4), so he must have been born in Babylon and come to Judah with Zerubbabel in 537 BC.

His father, Berechiah, probably died young, and his grandfather Iddo adopted him and raised him (Zech.

1:1; Ezra 6:14). Iddo was a priest (Neh. 12:1–4, 16), so Zechariah was both a prophet and a priest, like Ezekiel and John the Baptist. He began to preach about two months after Haggai began his ministry (Hag. 1:1) and a little over a month after the Jews resumed the work of rebuilding their temple (Hag. 1:15; Ezra 5:2).

Haggai's ministry was aimed at arousing the Jews to action, while Zechariah's messages were given for their encouragement (Zech. 1:13). Both prophets motivated the people by predicting future glory for the temple and future greatness for Israel. Zechariah has much to say about the future of Jerusalem and the coming of Messiah.

—*Be Heroic*, page 97

1. What are some of the encouragements Zechariah offered the Jews? How did he describe the coming Messiah? (See Zech. 3:8–9; 6:12–13; 9:9; 10:4; 11:12–13; 13:7; 14:1–4, 9, 16–17.) How might each of these descriptions have been meaningful to the formerly exiled Jews?

More to Consider: We know nothing about Zechariah's life or death, yet Zechariah's prophecy is quoted or alluded to at least forty-one times in the New Testament. Why doesn't the Bible tell us more about the man? What does this omission reveal about the way God chooses to reveal His truth?

2. Choose one verse or phrase from Zechariah 1—2 that stands out to you. This could be something you're intrigued by, something that makes you uncomfortable, something that puzzles you, something that resonates with you, or just something you want to examine further. Write that here.

Going Deeper

From the Commentary

A young preacher in his first pastorate phoned me for encouragement. "Most of the people in the church are older than I am," he said. "I wonder if they pay any attention to me. I feel like I'm out of place preaching to them."

Since I had faced the same situation in my first church, I was able to give him the same answer a veteran pastor gave me when I asked for help. "As long as you're delivering

God's message, don't worry about how old you are. When you open that Bible, you're over two thousand years old!"

Zechariah was a young man (Zech. 2:4) when God called him to minister to the struggling Jewish remnant trying to rebuild their temple in the ruined city of Jerusalem. The elder prophet Haggai had delivered two of his messages before Zechariah joined him in ministry, and the two of them served God together for a short time. Haggai had gotten the building program going again after a sixteen-year hiatus, and now Zechariah would encourage the people to finish their work.

—*Be Heroic*, page 101

3. Why is it notable that Zechariah was a young man? How did God encourage Zechariah in his ministry (Zech. 1:13, 17)? What are some ways Zechariah's life can serve as an inspiration to young leaders in churches today?

From the Commentary

A preacher's first sermon is usually difficult to deliver, but in Zechariah's case, his first message was doubly difficult because of the theme—repentance. God commanded His young servant to call the discouraged remnant to turn from their wicked ways and obey His Word. Zechariah boldly proclaimed what God told him to say, for, after all, the Lord couldn't bless His chosen people until they were clean in His sight. If Zechariah had wanted to quote a text for his sermon, it could well have been 2 Chronicles 7:14, a verse the Jewish people knew well.

Zechariah invited the people to look back and recall what their forefathers had done to provoke the Lord to anger and judgment (Zech. 1:2, 4). The Jewish people who had returned to the land knew their nation's history very well. They knew that God had sent prophet after prophet to plead with their forefathers to turn from idolatry and return to the Lord, but the nation had refused to listen.

Isaiah had warned the leaders that God would discipline the nation if they didn't change their ways (Isa. 2:6—3:26; 5:1–30; 29:1–14). Jeremiah wept as he warned Judah and Jerusalem that judgment was coming from the north (Babylon) and that the Jews would be exiled for seventy years (Jer. 1:13–16; 4:5–9; 6:22–26; 25:1–14). "And the LORD God of their fathers sent warnings to them by His messengers, rising up early and sending them, because He had compassion on His people and on His dwelling place. But they mocked the messengers of God, despised His words, and scoffed at His prophets, until the wrath of the LORD arose against His people, till there was no remedy" (2 Chron. 36:15–16 NKJV).

—Be Heroic, page 102

4. Review Zechariah 1:1–6. Why would this particular sermon have been difficult to deliver? What was the promise Zechariah offered in the course of his words? (See 1:3.) How is this promise still true for today's sometimes-wayward church?

From Today's World

We occasionally hear evangelists calling lost sinners to repent, and this is good and biblical. But we rarely hear preachers calling God's people to repent, even though this was the message of the prophets, John the Baptist, and Jesus. It's one thing to ask God to bless us but quite another to be the kind of people He can bless!

5. Why is calling for repentance such a controversial subject for today's church? What are the risks of being so bold in leadership? What does it look like for God's people to repent? Aren't they already redeemed? How can a call to repentance bring people closer to God?

From the Commentary

About three months later, during the night of February 15, 519 BC, Zechariah had a series of eight visions that God gave to encourage the remnant and motivate them to finish rebuilding the temple. These visions focus primarily on God's ministry to Israel and His judgment on the Gentile nations that have afflicted Israel.

In the first vision, the prophet saw a man on a red (bay) horse, leading an army astride red, brown, and white horses. This "man among the myrtle trees" was the Angel of the Lord (Zech. 1:11–13), the second person of the Godhead, who in Old Testament times made temporary preincarnate appearances on earth. As the Angel of the Lord, the Son of God appeared to Hagar (Gen. 16:7–14), Abraham (18; 22:11–18), Jacob (31:11, 13), Moses (Ex. 3), Gideon (Judg. 6:11–23), and Samson's parents (Judg. 13).

But there was also an "interpreting angel" there who explained various things to Zechariah (Zech. 1:9, 13–14, 19; 2:3; 4:1, 4–5; 5:10; 6:4–5). Ten times during these visions, Zechariah asked questions of this angel and received replies (1:9, 19, 21; 2:2; 4:4–5, 11–14; 5:5, 10–11; 6:4–8). "If any of you lacks wisdom, let him ask of God, who gives to all liberally and without reproach, and it will be given to him" (James 1:5 NKJV). "The secret of the LORD is with them that fear him; and he will show them his covenant" (Ps. 25:14).

—Be Heroic, pages 104–5

6. Review Zechariah 1:7–11. What did the Angel of the Lord teach Zechariah about the meaning of the horsemen? (See also 1 Kings 22:19; Job 1:6–7; 2:1–2; Dan. 7:10.) What did the messengers report about the Gentile nations? How was this a contrast to the way the Jewish remnant was feeling at the time?

From the Commentary

Over the centuries, the Jews have suffered repeatedly at the hands of many nations, and yet they have survived. But every nation that has sought to destroy the Jews has discovered the truth of God's promise to Abraham, "I will bless those who bless you, and I will curse him who curses you" (Gen. 12:3 NKJV).

That's the message of the second vision that God gave to Zechariah: The nations that have scattered the Jews will be terrified and thrown down by God's agents of judgment.

—*Be Heroic*, page 107

7. Review Zechariah 1:18–21. What is today's parallel for what God said in this passage? How does God bless those who bless His people and curse those who curse His people? Do we see the same kind of judgment today as we did in Zechariah's time? Why or why not? What's changed?

More to Consider: In Scripture, a horn is a symbol of power, especially the power of a nation or a ruler. (See Ps. 75:4–5; 89:17; 92:10; Jer. 48:25; Amos 6:13; Dan. 7:7–12; Rev. 17.) Why is that significant in Zechariah's vision? What might be a parallel symbol in today's world?

From the Commentary

The concept of four horns (nations) reminds us of Daniel's visions of the image (Dan. 2) and the beasts (Dan. 7), both of which speak of four empires: Babylon, Medo-Persia, Greece, and Rome. In 722 BC, Assyria devastated the northern kingdom of Israel, but God raised up Babylon to defeat Assyria (Jer. 25:9; 27:6) and eventually take Judah into captivity in 586. Babylon did indeed oppress the Jews, but then God raised up Cyrus to conquer Babylon in 539 (Isa. 44:28; 45:1); and in 538, He permitted the Jews to return to their land. The Persians were conquered by the Greeks under Alexander the Great, and Greece was conquered by Rome.

This scenario suggests that the "horns" also became "smiths" (craftsmen) as each empire conquered the previous oppressors.

—*Be Heroic*, page 107

8. How did this scenario in Zechariah 1:18–21 remind the Jews of God's providential care? Why might that have been of particular significance to the formerly exiled Jews? How does it also give believers today a sense of peace in light of the coming last days?

From the Commentary

The remnant that had returned to Judah was concerned about rebuilding the temple and restoring the city and the nation, but their work was extremely difficult. In this vision, God assured His people that He planned future glory and honor for them and their city when He Himself would come to dwell with them.

If a total stranger came into my house and began to measure the windows for curtains and the floor for carpeting, I'd probably ask him to leave. After all, you measure property that belongs to you, over which you have authority. When the prophet saw a man measuring Jerusalem, it was evidence that Jerusalem was God's city and that one day He would claim it and restore it in glory.

The man with the measuring line is evidently the Angel of the Lord, Israel's Messiah. Leaders and diplomats may debate over who shall control Jerusalem, but the Lord Jesus Christ has the final word. By measuring the city, He declares that it is His and He will accomplish His divine purposes for the city no matter what leaders and international assemblies may decide.

—*Be Heroic*, page 108

9. Review Zechariah 2:1–3. Why did the people constantly see the visions as evidence of a future Messiah? What does that say about their state of mind at the time? Their faith? How does today's church compare in how we look forward to the return of that Messiah? Why is it important for God's people to have a forward-thinking faith?

From the Commentary

> Promises like those in Zechariah 2:10–13 ought to make God's people "sing and rejoice" ("shout and be glad" NIV). Their Messiah will come and dwell with them, just as the glory of God had dwelt in the tabernacle and the temple. Ezekiel describes the new city and temple in Ezekiel 40—48 and closes his book by naming the glorious new city "Jehovah Shammah," which means "the Lord is there" (48:35). In that day, many Gentiles will trust in the Lord and be joined with Israel in the glorious kingdom over which Messiah will reign (Isa. 2:1–5; 19:23–25; 60:1–3; Zech. 8:20–23).
>
> Zechariah 2:12 is the only place in Scripture where Palestine is called "the holy land." That designation is often used today, but it really doesn't apply. The land will not be holy until Messiah cleanses the people and the land when He returns to reign (3:9). A fountain will be opened to wash away sin and uncleanness (13:1), and then the Jews shall be called "the holy people" (Isa. 62:12). That's something to shout about!
>
> —*Be Heroic*, pages 109–10

10. Why is Zechariah's message also something to make the nations of the world pause and consider? (See Zech. 2:13; Hab. 2:20; Zeph. 1:7.) When will God come to judge the nations of the earth? (See Jer. 30:7; Isa. 2:12; 13:6, 9; Joel 1:15; Zech. 14:1; Matt. 24:21; Rev. 6—19.) What does it mean

that God will rouse Himself from His holy dwelling (Zech. 2:13)? Why is this something for heathen nations to fear? Why don't they?

Looking Inward

Take a moment to reflect on all that you've explored thus far in this study of Zechariah 1—2. Review your notes and answers and think about how each of these things matters in your life today.

Tips for Small Groups: To get the most out of this section, form pairs or trios and have group members take turns answering these questions. Be honest and as open as you can in this discussion, but most of all, be encouraging and supportive of others. Be sensitive to those who are going through particularly difficult times, and don't press for people to speak if they're uncomfortable doing so.

11. What are some of the ways others have encouraged you in your faith? How do you encourage others? Why is encouragement so important for believers?

12. Have you ever been called to repent by a church leader? What was your initial reaction to that direct challenge? What does it mean for you to repent? How can repentance bring you closer to God?

13. How much time do you spend thinking about the end times? Is knowing the course of events important to you? Why or why not? How can you live in the now while still acknowledging and looking forward to God's plans for the future?

Going Forward

14. Think of one or two things that you have learned that you'd like to work on in the coming week. Remember that this is all about quality, not quantity. It's better to work on one specific area of life and do it well than to work on many and do poorly (or to be so overwhelmed that you simply don't try).

Is there something about which you want to repent? Be specific. Go back through Zechariah 1—2 and put a star next to the phrase or verse that is most encouraging to you. Consider memorizing this verse.

Real-Life Application Ideas: Zechariah delivered a powerful message calling God's people to repent, and then he became a great encourager to the somewhat-lost people. This week, consider the second part of that message and play the part of encourager wherever you go. Start first with your family members—look for practical ways to encourage them with notes, words, perhaps even small gifts. But don't neglect your workplace and social settings. Be sincere, and always listen for the Holy Spirit's guidance as you go about this very important work.

Seeking Help

15. Write a prayer below (or simply pray one in silence), inviting God to work on your mind and heart in those areas you've noted in the Going Forward section. Be honest about your desires and fears.

Notes for Small Groups:

- *Look for ways to put into practice the things you wrote in the Going Forward section. Talk with other group members about your ideas and commit to being accountable to one another.*

- *During the coming week, ask the Holy Spirit to continue to reveal truth to you from what you've read and studied.*

- *Before you start the next lesson, read Zechariah 3—6. For more in-depth lesson preparation, read chapters 8 and 9, "God and His Leaders" and "God and the Nations," in* Be Heroic.

Leaders and Nations

(ZECHARIAH 3—6)

Before you begin ...
- *Pray for the Holy Spirit to reveal truth and wisdom as you go through this lesson.*
- *Read Zechariah 3—6. This lesson references chapters 8 and 9 in* Be Heroic. *It will be helpful for you to have your Bible and a copy of the commentary available as you work through this lesson.*

Getting Started

From the Commentary

Haggai's first message (Hag. 1:1–11) and Zechariah's call to repentance (Zech. 1:1–6) are evidence that the spiritual level of the Jewish remnant was very low. Most of these people had been born in Babylon, where there wasn't much religious example or instruction to nourish their worship of Jehovah, and the difficult circumstances in their own land tested their faith greatly.

Joshua stood before the Lord as a representative of Israel, a people He had called to be a holy nation of priests (Ex. 19:5–6). He wore filthy clothes, not because he was sinful personally, but because the people had sinned and were unclean in God's sight. The emphasis here is on the nation collectively and not on Joshua individually, for both Joshua and Zerubbabel were "men symbolic of things to come" (Zech. 3:8 NIV). God had chosen Jerusalem and had plucked the Jews out of the fire of Babylonian captivity (v. 2).

—*Be Heroic*, page 114

1. How was what God did for Joshua in Zechariah 3:1–5 symbolic of what He would do for Israel (3:9)? Much of what fills all of these prophetic books is symbolic. How did the people know what the symbols meant for their time? How do we know what they mean for us today?

More to Consider: To "stand before the Lord" means to be in a place of service. (See Gen. 41:46; Deut. 10:8; 1 Sam. 16:21.) What would make the Jews "unclean" and therefore unfit to stand before the Lord? Why would God use such a vivid description (the word "filthy" denotes the worst kind of defilement for a Jew; see Zech. 3:3—4) to make such a point?

2. Choose one verse or phrase from Zechariah 3—6 that stands out to you. This could be something you're intrigued by, something that makes you uncomfortable, something that puzzles you, something that resonates with you, or just something you want to examine further. Write that here.

Going Deeper

From the Commentary

Christ's present ministry in heaven is twofold. He's our High Priest, interceding for us and giving us the grace we need for life and service here on earth (Heb. 4:14–16; 13:20–21), and He's our Advocate, representing us before the throne of God when we do sin (1 John 2:1–2). Don't get the erroneous idea that the Father yearns to punish us and the Son pleads with Him to change His mind, because that isn't the picture at all. The Father and the

Son both love us and want the best for us, but God can't
ignore our sins and still be a holy God.

—*Be Heroic*, page 115

3. How does Christ's present ministry explain why He took His wounds
back to heaven with Him (Luke 24:39–40; John 20:20, 25–27)? Why is
it important to our story that Jesus was "delivered over to death for our
sins and was raised to life for our justification" (Rom. 4:25)? Why was it
important for the returning Jewish remnant to see a future when there will
be no condemnation?

From the Commentary

The remarkable announcement in Zechariah 3:8–10
focuses on Jesus Christ and presents three different images
of the coming Messiah: the Priest, the Branch, and the
Stone. Zechariah will say more about the priest in 6:9–15.
In their priestly ministry, Joshua and his associates were
"symbolic of things to come" (3:8 NIV).

"The Branch" is an image of Messiah frequently found
in the prophets (Isa. 11:1–2). Here Messiah is called "my

servant the Branch" (Zech. 3:8). He is also "the Branch of the Lord" (Isa. 4:2), "the Branch of righteousness" raised up for David (Jer. 23:5; 33:15), and "the man whose name is The Branch" (Zech. 6:12–13). These four titles parallel four aspects of the person of Christ as seen in the four gospels:

Branch of righteousness for David—Matthew, Gospel of the King

My servant the Branch—Mark, Gospel of the Servant

The man whose name is The Branch—Luke, Gospel of the Son of Man

The Branch of the Lord—John, Gospel of the Son of God
—*Be Heroic*, pages 117–18

4. What does this parallel between Zechariah's message and the four gospels tell us about God's hand in Scripture? How does it solidify our belief that God is not only in charge of history but also actively inspiring the Scriptures themselves? How do Zechariah's visions help tie the Old and New Testaments together?

From the Commentary

> In the holy place of the tabernacle, in front of the veil and to the left of the altar of incense, stood a golden candlestick with seven branches (Ex. 25:31–40). At the end of each branch was a golden lamp, and it was the high priest's duty each morning and evening to trim the wicks and provide the oil needed to keep the lamp burning (Lev. 24:2–4). This candlestick provided light in the Holy Place so the priests could see to burn the incense on the golden altar each morning and evening (Ex. 30:7–8).
>
> But the candlestick that Zechariah saw was totally unlike the one Moses had put into the tabernacle. Along with the seven branches and lamps, this candlestick had a bowl at the top into which olive oil dripped from two olive trees (Zech. 4:3), which symbolized Joshua and Zerubbabel (v. 14). The candlestick also had seven pipes going from the bowl to each lamp, making a total of forty-nine pipes. No priest had to provide the oil because it was always coming from the trees. Seven pipes to each lamp assured an ample supply of fuel to keep the lights burning.
>
> —*Be Heroic*, pages 119–20

5. In what ways was the lampstand in the tabernacle symbolic of the Messiah? (See John 8:12.) How might the tabernacle candlestick represent Israel, the nation God had chosen to be a light in a spiritually dark world? (See Isa. 60:1–3; 62:1.) What is the significance of the "light in a dark

world" symbolism for today's church? Where is the power source for our light? (See Matt. 5:14–16; Phil. 2:14–16.)

From the Commentary

> When Solomon built the temple that the Babylonians destroyed, he had almost unlimited resources at his disposal. His father, David, had fought many battles and collected spoil to be used in building the temple (1 Chron. 26:20, 27–28), but the remnant didn't have an army. Solomon was monarch of a powerful kingdom that ruled over many Gentile nations and took tribute from them, but the Jews in Zechariah's day had no such authority.
>
> That's why God said to them through His prophet, "Not by might, nor by power, but by my Spirit" (Zech. 4:6). The word *might* refers to military might, what people can do together, but the remnant had no army. "Power" refers to the strength of the individual, but Zerubbabel's strength was no doubt waning. "Don't be discouraged!" was the prophet's message. "The Spirit of God will enable us to do what an army could never do!" Had they forgotten what

Haggai said to them? "My Spirit remains among you. Do not fear" (Hag. 2:5 NIV).

—Be Heroic, pages 120–21

6. There are three ways in which we can attempt to do the work of God: We can trust our own strength and wisdom, we can borrow the resources of the world, or we can depend on the power of God. How did the Jews attempt each of these approaches? How do we do the same thing today? What is the biggest difference between the first two and the third? (See 1 Cor. 3:12–15.) How do we access the power of God in the everyday?

From the Commentary

The prophet describes three key events that give evidence that the God of Abraham, Isaac, and Jacob is indeed "the Lord of the whole earth." The first is the cleansing of the land (Zech. 5:1–11).

The vision of the flying scroll and the vision of the ephah focus primarily on the land of Israel. In both of them, God performs a cleansing operation and deals with the sins of the nation.

The prophet saw a large open scroll, fifteen feet by thirty feet, floating through the air, with writing on both sides. On one side he read the third commandment against taking God's name in vain (Ex. 20:7), and on the other side he read the eighth commandment against stealing (v. 15).

This scroll represented the law of God that brings a curse on all who disobey it, and that includes all of us (Deut. 27:26; Gal. 3:10–12), because nobody can fully obey God's law. For that matter, the law was never given to save people (Gal. 2:16, 21; 3:21) but to reveal that people need to be saved, "for by the law is the knowledge of sin" (Rom. 3:20).

—*Be Heroic*, pages 127–28

7. Out of the Ten Commandments, why did the Lord select the two that forbid stealing and swearing falsely? (See Hag. 1:1–11; Mal. 3:7–15.) In what ways is the third commandment central to the commands about relating to God? In what ways is the eighth commandment central to the commands about relating to other people? Why was obedience so important for the Jewish people at this moment in history? Why is it important for us today?

From the Commentary

> Not only will individual sins and sinners be judged, but also wickedness itself will be removed from the land. In this vision, wickedness is personified by a woman, because the Hebrew word for "wickedness" is feminine. The ephah was a common measure in Israel, but no ephah would be large enough to house a person, so, like the huge scroll, this was a special ephah. The woman attempted to get out of the ephah, so a heavy lead cover was put on the ephah to keep her in. A talent of lead would weigh from seventy-five to one hundred pounds.
>
> The prophet then saw two other women, but they had wings! With the help of the wind, they lifted up the basket and its contents, plus the heavy lead cover, and carried it in the air to Babylon. Although angels are actually sexless (Matt. 22:30), in Scripture they are generally depicted as male, so these two women were special agents of the Lord created just for this particular task. They took the ephah and the woman to Shinar (Babylon, Dan. 1:2) and put the ephah on a base in a special house.
>
> —*Be Heroic*, pages 129–30

8. In order to understand this vision in Zechariah 5, we must ask ourselves, "What did the Jews bring to their land from Babylon when they returned after their captivity?" (Hint: It's not idolatry.) In what ways might the woman in the ephah represent the spirit of competitive commercialism? Why would that be of any concern? What are the dangers of commercialism

and consumerism? How was God addressing these in this vision? How are they applicable today?

More to Consider: The ancient city of Babylon is first mentioned in Genesis 10:10 as a part of Nimrod's empire. Nimrod is called "a mighty warrior on the earth" and "a mighty hunter" (Gen. 10:8–9). This is the picture of a conquering despot, forging himself a kingdom at any cost and defying the Lord in the process. The famous Tower of Babel was built in Shinar as an attempt to exalt people and dethrone God (Gen. 11:1–9). How does this help us understand why Babylon symbolizes the world's enmity against God? (See also Rev. 17—18 and the parallel in Jer. 50—51.) In what ways might the Jews have caught the "virus" of consumerism during their exile in Babylon? What is the overarching message to God's people about the dangers of wealth and consumerism?

From the Commentary

The images in the vision found in Zechariah 6:1–8 are similar to those described in Zechariah 1:7–17, but the details are significantly different. The emphasis here is on the horses and chariots rather than the riders, and their ministry is that of accomplishing God's purposes rather than reporting on conditions in the Gentile world. In the first vision, there were many horses and riders, but here, there are only four chariots, each with their horses.

The four chariots with their horses represented the "four spirits" from God, that is, four angels (Heb. 1:14) assigned to different parts of the world to do God's bidding. "The chariots of God are twenty thousand, even thousands of angels" (Ps. 68:17). The presence of chariots suggests battle, and this implies judgment. "For behold, the LORD will come with fire and with His chariots, like a whirlwind, to render [bring down, NIV] His anger with fury, and His rebuke with flames of fire" (Isa. 66:15 NKJV).

If the horses' colors are significant, then Revelation 6:1–8 can assist us. The red horses symbolize war; the black horses, famine; and the white horses, death. There are no dappled horses in the vision John had in Revelation 6, but they could well symbolize plagues. During the "day of the Lord," God will use wars, famines, plagues, and death to punish the nations of the earth.

—*Be Heroic*, pages 131–32

9. Horses and chariots were the advanced military hardware of biblical times. Why were horses used so often as symbols in Scripture? What might be a parallel to those horses in today's world? What was the purpose of using symbolic language in this vision versus just telling the people directly

what it all meant? How might they grow in their relationship with the Lord as they tried to understand the meaning here?

From the Commentary

> The eight visions came to an end, but there was yet another message from God to His servant. In the visions, God had assured His people that He would cleanse them and protect them from their enemies. But there was a message for the future as well. During the "day of the Lord," the nations would be punished for their sins, but Israel would be delivered. At the climax of that day, Messiah would return, the Jews would see Him and trust Him, and the nation would be cleansed. Then Messiah would be crowned as King-Priest to reign over His righteous kingdom (Zech. 9—14).
>
> —*Be Heroic*, page 133

10. Review Zechariah 6:9–15. How was what happened here to the high priest a picture of the Messiah? How did all the visions present a vivid panorama of God's plans for Israel? What would be the ultimate result of

those visions? How do these prophecies offer an appropriate answer to the phrase "your kingdom come" in the Lord's Prayer?

Looking Inward

Take a moment to reflect on all that you've explored thus far in this study of Zechariah 3—6. Review your notes and answers and think about how each of these things matters in your life today.

Tips for Small Groups: To get the most out of this section, form pairs or trios and have group members take turns answering these questions. Be honest and as open as you can in this discussion, but most of all, be encouraging and supportive of others. Be sensitive to those who are going through particularly difficult times, and don't press for people to speak if they're uncomfortable doing so.

11. How do you approach the myriad of symbolism in the Bible? Are you overwhelmed by it? Confused by it? Do you try to understand every subtle implication or just get the basic gist of the meaning? What are some modern symbols that help you understand God and His plan for your life?

12. How do you access God's power in your everyday life? Do you know when God is "fueling" an aspect of your life? Explain. What makes it difficult to trust God's power? Why is trusting God essential?

13. What comes to mind when you pray "Your kingdom come"? What does God's kingdom look like to you? In what ways are you already in God's kingdom? In what ways is it yet to come?

Going Forward

14. Think of one or two things that you have learned that you'd like to work on in the coming week. Remember that this is all about quality, not quantity. It's better to work on one specific area of life and do it well than to work on many and do poorly (or to be so overwhelmed that you simply don't try).

Do you want to have more confidence when you pray "Your kingdom come"? Be specific. Go back through Zechariah 3—6 and put a star next to the phrase or verse that is most encouraging to you. Consider memorizing this verse.

Real-Life Application Ideas: Zechariah is a book loaded with symbolism. This week, spend your quiet time studying the various symbols you find in Old Testament prophecies. Choose three or four passages and look them up in scholarly commentaries, with the goal of better understanding the context in which they were written. There are always potentially two meanings for each prophecy in Scripture— the meaning that's meant for the people to whom the prophecy was originally directed and the meaning for us today. Seek to understand the former; then ask God to reveal the latter in your life and what that means for your daily living. To add value to this study, have each member of your small group pick a different passage to study. Then get together to share a meal and a time for examining the importance of symbolism for God's people then and now.

Seeking Help

15. Write a prayer below (or simply pray one in silence), inviting God to work on your mind and heart in those areas you've noted in the Going Forward section. Be honest about your desires and fears.

Notes for Small Groups:

- *Look for ways to put into practice the things you wrote in the Going Forward section. Talk with other group members about your ideas and commit to being accountable to one another.*
- *During the coming week, ask the Holy Spirit to continue to reveal truth to you from what you've read and studied.*
- *Before you start the next lesson, read Zechariah 7—11. For more in-depth lesson preparation, read chapters 10 and 11, "Truth, Traditions, and Promises" and "Messiah, the Shepherd-King," in* Be Heroic.

Promises
(ZECHARIAH 7—11)

Before you begin ...
- *Pray for the Holy Spirit to reveal truth and wisdom as you go through this lesson.*
- *Read Zechariah 7—11. This lesson references chapters 10 and 11 in* Be Heroic. *It will be helpful for you to have your Bible and a copy of the commentary available as you work through this lesson.*

Getting Started

From the Commentary

Tradition is a useful and necessary social practice. It helps to tie generations together and keep society moving in a united way. Whether the traditions involve the way we eat and dress, how we treat our parents and family, the way we move from childhood into maturity, or the way we choose a job or a mate, tradition helps to stabilize things and guide us in making acceptable choices. But sometimes tradition creates problems, especially when the times change radically and people don't want to change with the times.

Almost two years had elapsed since the crowning of Joshua, and the work of rebuilding the temple had gone on steadily. In another three years, the temple would be completed and dedicated. While we have no recorded messages from Zechariah during that time, certainly he was ministering to the people and encouraging the workers in their important task.

The law of Moses required the Jews to observe only one national fast, and that was on the annual Day of Atonement (Lev. 23:16–32). Of course, individual Jews could fast from time to time as they felt led, but this wasn't required of the entire nation.

To commemorate events surrounding the destruction of Jerusalem and the temple, four new fasts had been added to the religious calendar by the Jewish exiles in Babylon (see Zech. 8:19): one in the tenth month, when the Babylonians had begun the siege of the city; another in the fourth month, when the city walls had been broken through; one in the fifth month, when the temple was burned; and the fourth in the seventh month, when the Jewish governor Gedaliah had been assassinated (see Jer. 41).

—Be Heroic, pages 139–40

1. Review Zechariah 7:1–7. The significant question here was "Now that the temple was being rebuilt, was it necessary to continue the fast in the

fifth month that commemorated the burning of the temple?" What was Zechariah's response? Why didn't he offer a direct answer? (He later revealed God's will in 8:9.) Why did he first deal with other things the people did?

More to Consider: In true rabbinical fashion, Zechariah answered their question by asking some questions. What questions did he ask? Why was this "answering a question with a question" approach so common in the Jewish culture? What does this approach teach the people asking the question?

2. Choose one verse or phrase from Zechariah 7—11 that stands out to you. This could be something you're intrigued by, something that makes you uncomfortable, something that puzzles you, something that resonates with you, or just something you want to examine further. Write that here.

Going Deeper

From the Commentary

> In Zechariah 7:8–14, the prophet reminded the people of
> the way their forefathers routinely practiced their religion
> but failed to hear God's Word and obey it from their
> hearts. That was the reason Jerusalem and the temple
> had been destroyed. Their religion was just a part of their
> lives; it wasn't the very heart of their lives. They could
> go to the temple and piously present their prayers and
> sacrifices, but then leave the temple to break God's law,
> worship idols, and abuse other people.
>
> Through the prophets, the Lord had called the people to
> practice justice, but the leaders had continued to exploit
> the people for personal gain. The rulers of the nation had
> ignored the law of Moses and refused to show compassion
> toward the poor, the widows and orphans, and the aliens
> in the land (Ex. 22:22–24; Deut. 10:18–22; Amos 2:6–8;
> 5:11–12, 21–24). God wasn't interested in their sacrifices
> and prayers so much as the obedience of their hearts.
>
> —*Be Heroic*, page 142

3. Why is compassion for the poor such a persistent theme in the prophets'
messages? Why is justice such a persistent theme? In what ways are these
still issues that God's people need to deal with? How is this a challenge for
today's church?

From the Commentary

God's people don't live on explanations; they live on promises. Faith and hope are nourished by the promises of God given to us in the Scriptures. That explains why Zechariah dropped the discussion of the traditions and delivered a new message from the Lord. In this message, he focused the people's eyes of faith on the future and shared some wonderful promises to encourage them.

God affirmed His jealous love and concern for Zion, just as He had done earlier (Zech. 1:14). He promises that Jerusalem will be rebuilt and become a wholly different city, dedicated to truth and holiness. This promise will be fulfilled when Jesus Christ returns to earth to establish His kingdom (Isa. 1:26; 2:3; 60:14; 62:12).

—*Be Heroic*, page 144

4. Note the uses of the phrase "This is what the LORD Almighty says" in Zechariah 8. Why is this wording significant? How is the city described in Zechariah 8? What is God's emphasis here? Why were safety and comfort so important to the Jews at this point in their history? How is this same safety and comfort promised for heaven important to believers today?

From the Commentary

Haggai had rebuked the Jewish remnant because the people weren't faithful to the Lord in their stewardship (Hag. 1). Instead of honoring the Lord and building His house, they built their own houses first, and for this sin, God disciplined them. The weather turned bad, their crops failed, and the economy became worse and worse. God wasn't being unkind to His people; He was only being true to His covenant (Deut. 28:38–46).

But now the land would be refreshed by the Lord and the crops would grow abundantly. Laborers would get their wages, and their money would be sufficient to pay their bills. The Lord would send the promised rain (Deut. 28:11–12), and the other nations would witness the blessing of the Lord on His people. Instead of being a reproach, Israel would become a witness to the glory of the Lord.

While this promise of material blessing was given primarily to the remnant in Zechariah's day, it has its application to the future regathered and restored nation. God promises that "the desert shall rejoice, and blossom as the rose" (Isa. 35:1) in the kingdom of Messiah.

—*Be Heroic*, pages 145–46

5. Why would the mention of material blessing be significant to the people in Zechariah's day? What is a parallel to this for today's believers? When does God trust His people with material blessings? How are they a way

of saying "You're maturing in godliness"? Is poverty a sign that God has forsaken His people? Explain. (See also the book of Job.)

From the Commentary

> God called Abraham and established the nation of Israel so His people would witness to the Gentiles and lead them to faith in the true God (Gen. 12:1–3). In setting apart one nation, God was seeking to reach a whole world. Many of the great events in Jewish history recorded in Scripture had behind them a witness to "the whole world": the plagues of Egypt (Ex. 9:16); the conquest of Canaan (Josh. 4:23–24); God's blessing of the nation (Deut. 28:9–11); and even the building of the temple (1 Kings 8:42–43). When David killed Goliath, he announced that God would give him victory so "that all the earth may know that there is a God in Israel" (1 Sam. 17:46).
>
> But Israel failed in her mission to the Gentiles.
>
> —*Be Heroic*, pages 147–48

6. How did the Israelites fail in their mission to the Gentiles? Why did this matter? How did their failure set the table for Jesus' role in bringing God's truth to the nations?

From the Commentary

> In the last half of his book, Zechariah presents two oracles ("burdens") that focus on the first and second advents of the coming Messiah. These six chapters comprise one of the greatest concentrations of messianic truth found anywhere in Scripture, but the truth is always related to God's purposes for His people Israel.
>
> —*Be Heroic*, page 151

7. Zechariah revealed the Messiah as the humble King, the loving Shepherd, the mighty Warrior, the gracious Savior, and the righteous Ruler who will reign on earth as King and Priest. How would each of these pictures of the Messiah have given the returning remnant hope? How do these same pictures give us hope today?

From the Commentary

The coming of God's Son to this earth wasn't heaven's "Plan B" or a hasty decision by the Father after our first parents sinned. The plan of redemption was settled in eternity, before there ever was a creation. The coming of the Lamb of God was "foreordained before the foundation of the world" (1 Peter 1:20), for He was "the Lamb slain from the foundation of the world" (Rev. 13:8).

—*Be Heroic*, pages 151–52

8. Review Zechariah 9:1–9. How does this passage help us understand the "long plan" for redemption? Why is it so important that God had this plan long before the creation of humankind? What does this teach us about God? About His patience with His creation? About His love for us?

More to Consider: The promise in Zechariah 9:8 goes far beyond the time of Alexander, for it states that God is always protecting His people and His house. How does this promise line up with the fact that the Jewish nation still suffered on many more occasions after the time of Alexander? How does this promise speak to the future age? How do we still count on that promise today?

From the Commentary

The entire age of the church fits between Zechariah 9:9 and 9:10, just as it does between Isaiah 9:6 and 7 and after the comma in Isaiah 61:2. The prophet is now writing about what will happen when Jesus comes to earth to defeat His enemies and establish His kingdom. At His first advent, He rode a humble donkey, but at His second advent, He will ride a white horse and lead the armies of heaven (Rev. 19:11–21).

—*Be Heroic*, page 154

9. How does the entire age of the church fit between Zechariah 9:9 and 9:10? How do we know that this section of Zechariah is speaking about the second advent? How do these verses line up with the truth of Jesus' promises in the Gospels?

From the Commentary

The two chapters we've just surveyed (Zech. 9—10) indicate that Israel will be in trouble in the last days until their Messiah comes to rescue them, cleanse them, and give them a kingdom. How did they get into this trouble?

During the time of David and Solomon, Israel was the most powerful nation on earth, with wealth and resources beyond measure. After Solomon's death, the nation divided into two kingdoms, Israel and Judah. Israel, the northern kingdom, began to deteriorate, so God sent the Assyrians to conquer them and scatter them. Judah had a series of godless kings, so God sent the Babylonians to take Judah captive.

Seventy years later, a small band of Jews returned to their land to rebuild their temple. Life was difficult, and the nation had none of its former glory, but over the years they persisted and restored the temple and the city. Then their Messiah, Jesus Christ, came to them, and they rejected Him and asked their Roman rulers to have Him crucified. About forty years later, in AD 70, the Roman armies came and destroyed Jerusalem and the temple and scattered the Jews to the nations of the world. Because they didn't receive their own Messiah, they have been a scattered people ever since.

Zechariah 11 explains the nation's rejection of the true Messiah and how they will accept a false messiah, the Antichrist, who will appear at the end of the age and deceive the whole world. The key image in the chapter is that of the shepherd, and three different shepherds are presented.

—Be Heroic, page 158

10. Describe the three different shepherds presented in Zechariah 11 (read carefully verses 1–3, then 4–14 and 15–17). Why did Zechariah use the image of a shepherd to describe the Messiah? How does this match what we find in the New Testament? What makes each of these descriptions important to our understanding of the Messiah?

Looking Inward

Take a moment to reflect on all that you've explored thus far in this study of Zechariah 7—11. Review your notes and answers and think about how each of these things matters in your life today.

Tips for Small Groups: To get the most out of this section, form pairs or trios and have group members take turns answering these questions. Be honest and as open as you can in this discussion, but most of all, be encouraging and supportive of others. Be sensitive to those who are going through particularly difficult times, and don't press for people to speak if they're uncomfortable doing so.

11. Think about a time when you really wanted to hear God's will on something. What was it like to wait for God's answer? Did you ever hear God's answer? Explain. What role might the state of your heart have played in God's response (or delay) to that desire?

12. What are some of the material blessings God has given you? What does this tell you about your relationship with God? Do you ever feel like you "deserve" material blessings? If so, what prompts that way of thinking?

13. What are you most looking forward to about the second coming of Christ? What are some things you can do today to prepare for that time?

Going Forward

14. Think of one or two things that you have learned that you'd like to work on in the coming week. Remember that this is all about quality, not quantity. It's better to work on one specific area of life and do it well than to work on many and do poorly (or to be so overwhelmed that you simply don't try).

Do you want to better understand why and how God gives material blessings? Be specific. Go back through Zechariah 7—11 and put a star next to the phrase or verse that is most encouraging to you. Consider memorizing this verse.

Real-Life Application Ideas: The second coming of Christ is the basis for much of our hope, but certainly not all of it. God has already redeemed us in Jesus' life, death, and resurrection. So we're already living in God's kingdom while awaiting a future in which God's final plan will be revealed. Think this week about the kingdom of today rather than focusing on the promise of heaven. Where do you see God's hand in today's world? Look for God in the everyday, even in how He works through you, and each time you see a glimpse of the kingdom, offer thanks. Make this a week of worship and praise for all that you have been granted while your feet are still planted.

Seeking Help

15. Write a prayer below (or simply pray one in silence), inviting God to work on your mind and heart in those areas you've noted in the Going Forward section. Be honest about your desires and fears.

Notes for Small Groups:

- *Look for ways to put into practice the things you wrote in the Going Forward section. Talk with other group members about your ideas and commit to being accountable to one another.*

- *During the coming week, ask the Holy Spirit to continue to reveal truth to you from what you've read and studied.*

- *Before you start the next lesson, read Zechariah 12—14. For more in-depth lesson preparation, read chapter 12, "Redeemed, Refined, and Restored," in* Be Heroic.

Restoration
(ZECHARIAH 12—14)

Before you begin ...
- *Pray for the Holy Spirit to reveal truth and wisdom as you go through this lesson.*
- *Read Zechariah 12—14. This lesson references chapter 12 in* Be Heroic. *It will be helpful for you to have your Bible and a copy of the commentary available as you work through this lesson.*

Getting Started

From the Commentary

In this second oracle, Zechariah takes us to the end times. He describes the Gentile nations attacking Jerusalem, the Jews experiencing severe trials ("the time of Jacob's trouble"), and then the Lord returning in power and great glory to deliver His people and establish the promised kingdom. What an exciting scenario it is! But it isn't fiction; it's God's own Word, and it will come to pass.

—*Be Heroic*, page 165

1. Underline every instance of the phrase "on that day" or "in that day" in Zechariah 12—14. What is "that day"? (See Joel 3:9–16; Zeph. 1.) Why did Zechariah refer to it so often? What is it about this one day that makes it worthy of such attention in these last three chapters? Is there a danger in putting too much emphasis on this? Explain.

2. Choose one verse or phrase from Zechariah 12—14 that stands out to you. This could be something you're intrigued by, something that makes you uncomfortable, something that puzzles you, something that resonates with you, or just something you want to examine further. Write that here.

Going Deeper

From the Commentary

> Jerusalem is mentioned fifty-two times in the book of
> Zechariah, and twenty-two of these references are in the
> final three chapters. In the first chapter of his prophecy,
> Zechariah told us that God was "jealous for Jerusalem
> and for Zion with a great jealousy" (1:14). This statement
> reveals the yearning heart of a loving Father for His first-
> born (Ex. 4:22) and the desire of a faithful Husband for
> His unfaithful bride (Jer. 2:2; 3:2).
>
> —*Be Heroic*, pages 165–66

3. How do the last chapters of Zechariah support the truth that God's
timing and ours don't always line up? Why was it so important for the
people in Zechariah's time to look forward to a hopeful future? What had
their recent experiences in Babylon taught them about God's "mysterious
ways"?

More to Consider: Why did Zechariah describe Jerusalem's situation "on that day" with the images of a cup and a rock? (See Ps. 75:8; Isa. 51:17, 21–23; Jer. 25:15–28; Ezek. 23:31–33; Hab. 2:16; Rev. 14:10; 16:19; 18:6.) How did the nations plan to "swallow up" Jerusalem? What would be the result of those attempts, according to Zechariah?

From the Commentary

Our Lord ascended to heaven from the Mount of Olives (Acts 1:9–12), and when He returns to earth, He will stand on the Mount of Olives and cause a great earthquake to change the terrain (Isa. 29:6; Rev. 16:18–19). This will create a new valley that will provide an escape route for many of the people. There will also be changes in the heavens so that the day will be neither light nor darkness, morning nor evening (see Isa. 60:19–20).

"The LORD is a man of war," sang the Jews after they were delivered from Egypt (Ex. 15:3), but this aspect of Christ's character and ministry is ignored, if not opposed, by people today. In their quest for world peace, some denominations have removed the "militant songs" from their hymnals, so that a new generation is growing up knowing nothing about "fighting the good fight of faith" or worshipping a Savior who will one day meet the nations of the world in battle (Rev. 19:11–21).

—*Be Heroic*, page 167

4. Review Zechariah 14:3–7. Before the Israelites entered the Promised Land, Moses promised them that the Lord would fight for them (Deut. 1:30; 3:22). How did this promise also apply to the situation the Jews found themselves in after their exile in Babylon? How does Isaiah 42:13 speak to the promise for the Israelites' future? What does this entire story teach us about God's long-suffering nature? Why would God choose to be patient with nations that defy Him?

From Today's World

The early church, particularly in Paul's time, was focused on sharing the good news of Jesus' love and sacrifice and the promise of redemption. But the early believers also carried with them the anticipation of Jesus' "soon return," having been so close to His time on earth. Over the years, the church has had seasons when it has focused on the second coming and seasons when the second coming has all but disappeared from the lexicon. Of course this varies from church tradition to church tradition, but in today's world, there seems to be a clearer divide between those who are focused on the signs of Jesus' soon return and those who have little interest in considering the second coming, whether that's because they focus on immediate concerns or because they deem it of little significance in the bigger scheme of things.

5. What is so appealing about the second-coming message? How can it bring people to Christ? What are the dangers of focusing too much on that aspect of our faith story? Is it important to watch for the signs of the end times? Why or why not?

From the Commentary

> In delivering Israel from her enemies, our Lord's ultimate goal is more than their national preservation, for their spiritual restoration is uppermost in His heart. He wants to reveal Himself to them and establish the kind of relationship that was impossible in previous centuries because of their unbelief.
>
> Repentance isn't something we work up ourselves; it's a gift from God as we hear His Word and recognize His grace (Acts 5:31; 11:18; 2 Tim. 2:25).
>
> —*Be Heroic*, page 168

6. Review Zechariah 12:10–14. How is repentance a gift from God? In what ways will God pouring His Spirit upon the people of Israel (Joel 2:28–29)

help them realize their sins? How will this help them see their Messiah, whom their nation crucified (Ps. 22:16; Isa. 53:5; John 19:34, 37)?

From the Commentary

> Isaiah had admonished the nation, "Wash yourselves, make yourselves clean; put away the evil of your doings from before My eyes" (Isa. 1:16 NKJV), but they refused to listen. Jeremiah had pleaded with his people, "O Jerusalem, wash your heart from wickedness, that you may be saved" (Jer. 4:14 NKJV), but they wouldn't obey. But now, in response to Israel's repentance and faith, the Lord will wash them clean! This forgiveness is part of the new covenant that God promised to His people (Jer. 31:31–34): "For I will forgive their wickedness and will remember their sins no more" (v. 34 NIV).
>
> William Cowper based his hymn "There Is a Fountain Filled with Blood" on Zechariah 13:1, for it's the sacrifice of Christ that atones for sin. The Jews could cleanse their external ceremonial uncleanness by washing in water, but for internal cleansing, the sinful hearts of men and women can be cleansed only by the blood of the Savior

(Lev. 16:30; 17:11). "And He Himself is the propitiation for our sins, and not for ours only but also for the whole world" (1 John 2:2 NKJV).

—*Be Heroic*, page 169

7. Review Zechariah 13:1–6. Why was the symbolism of cleansing so meaningful to the Jews? How did Zechariah use this symbolism here? What was the "spirit of impurity" or "unclean spirit" that caused people to turn from God (v. 2)?

From the Commentary

The image in Zechariah 13:8–9 reminds us of the value God puts on His people Israel: They are like gold and silver that need to be refined in the furnace of affliction. This had been their experience in Egypt (Deut. 4:20) and in Babylon (Isa. 48:10), but "the time of Jacob's trouble" (Jer. 30:7) will be their most difficult "furnace experience."

—*Be Heroic*, page 170

8. Why would the imagery of refining gold be meaningful to the people during Zechariah's time? How might the last days be like the refinement process a goldsmith uses? Is it necessary to believe in the tribulation (and other hotly debated end-time events) in order to live a life of faith? How can studying these events and their significance help us grow closer to God?

More to Consider: Before we leave this section, we need to see the spiritual application for God's people today. Certainly the church is a defiled people who need to repent and be cleansed, and the promise of forgiveness is still valid (1 John 1:9). And God often still has to put us through the furnace of suffering before we'll call on Him and seek His face (Heb. 12:3–11; 1 Peter 4:12). How would following the instructions of 2 Chronicles 7:14 cleanse the church and prepare the way to bring healing to the land?

From the Commentary

"And the LORD shall be king over all the earth: in that day shall there be one LORD, and his name one" (Zech. 14:9). After the nations have been punished and Israel has been purified, the Lord will establish His righteous kingdom and reign on David's throne (Luke 1:32–33; Rev. 17:14; 19:16). His reign will be universal ("over all the earth"), He will be the only God worshipped, and His name will be the only name honored. (See Ps. 72; Jer. 30:7–9.)

—*Be Heroic*, page 171

9. According to Zechariah 14:9–11, 16–21, what will happen when the King reigns supremely? How does the modern church celebrate this future event? How should we?

From the Commentary

Zechariah's book begins with a call to repentance, but it ends with a vision of a holy nation and a glorious kingdom. Zechariah was one of God's heroes who ministered at a difficult time and in a difficult place, but he encouraged God's people by showing them visions of what God has planned for their future. God is still jealous over Jerusalem and the Jewish people, and He will fulfill His promises.

—*Be Heroic*, page 174

10. How is Zechariah's book similar in content and organization to the message in the New Testament? What is the call to repentance found in the Gospels? What is the vision of the future found in the New Testament? How can Zechariah's visions inspire us as we seek to live out the Great Commission?

Looking Inward

Take a moment to reflect on all that you've explored thus far in this study of Zechariah 12—14. Review your notes and answers and think about how each of these things matters in your life today.

> *Tips for Small Groups: To get the most out of this section, form pairs or trios and have group members take turns answering these questions. Be honest and as open as you can in this discussion, but most of all, be encouraging and supportive of others. Be sensitive to those who are going through particularly difficult times, and don't press for people to speak if they're uncomfortable doing so.*

11. How often do you focus on the second coming of Christ? Do you hope Jesus will come soon? Why or why not? This is a difficult question to answer honestly, of course. Why would anyone want to delay Christ's

return? But it might reveal what's going on in your heart—the good and the not so good—so it's a valid and important question.

12. How do you see your value to God? Do you see yourself as "gold and silver"? Explain. How might understanding yourself as God's "treasure" help you live out your faith in everyday life? How can that knowledge help you through trying times?

13. What practical actions does a book like Zechariah inspire you to take? While the prophecies were clearly meant for a moment in history, their implications and meaning throw a long shadow. What are some ways that shadow touches your life?

Going Forward

14. Think of one or two things that you have learned that you'd like to work on in the coming week. Remember that this is all about quality, not quantity. It's better to work on one specific area of life and do it well than to work on many and do poorly (or to be so overwhelmed that you simply don't try).

Do you want to live with more hope, in light of the second coming? Be specific. Go back through Zechariah 12—14 and put a star next to the phrase or verse that is most encouraging to you. Consider memorizing this verse.

Real-Life Application Ideas: Zechariah was speaking to a people who had suffered mightily over many generations, often because of their own failure to trust God. He offered them both a challenge (repent) and a hope. This week, focus on that hope. Spend your quiet times reflecting on God's promise to cleanse the nations and return for His people. Don't get hung up on the theology of this—just inhale God's promise of peace and exhale your thanks. Sometimes the simplest acts make the biggest difference in our attitudes and actions.

Seeking Help

15. Write a prayer below (or simply pray one in silence), inviting God to work on your mind and heart in those areas you've noted in the Going Forward section. Be honest about your desires and fears.

Notes for Small Groups:

- *Look for ways to put into practice the things you wrote in the Going Forward section. Talk with other group members about your ideas and commit to being accountable to one another.*

- *During the coming week, ask the Holy Spirit to continue to reveal truth to you from what you've read and studied.*

Summary and Review

Notes for Small Groups: This session is a summary and review of this book. Because of that, it is shorter than the previous lessons. If you are using this in a small-group setting, consider combining this lesson with a time of fellowship or a shared meal.

Before you begin ...
- *Pray for the Holy Spirit to reveal truth and wisdom as you go through this lesson.*
- *Briefly review the notes you made in the previous sessions. You will refer back to previous sections throughout this bonus lesson.*

Looking Back

1. Over the past eight lessons, you've examined three minor prophets. What expectations did you bring to this study? In what ways were those expectations met?

2. What is the most significant personal discovery you've made from this study?

3. What surprised you most about Ezra? Haggai? Zechariah? What, if anything, troubled you?

Progress Report

4. Take a few moments to review the Going Forward sections of the previous lessons. How would you rate your progress for each of the things you chose to work on? What adjustments, if any, do you need to make to continue on the path toward spiritual maturity?

5. In what ways have you grown closer to Christ during this study? Take a moment to celebrate those things. Then think of areas where you feel you still need to grow and note those here. Make plans to revisit this study in a few weeks to review your growing faith.

Things to Pray About

6. These prophetic books are about God's promises to His people and the heroism that it often takes to seek God in a land that doesn't see Him as sovereign. As you reflect on what it means to be heroic, ask God to lead you to wisdom on what that means for your daily life of faith.

7. The messages in these books include trust, patience, heroism, God's long-suffering, repentance, and hope. Spend time praying for each of these topics.

8. Whether you've been studying this in a small group or on your own, there are many other Christians working through the very same issues you discovered when examining these books of the Bible. Take time to pray for them, that God would reveal truth, that the Holy Spirit would guide you, and that each person might grow in spiritual maturity according to God's will.

A Blessing of Encouragement

Studying the Bible is one of the best ways to learn how to be more like Christ. Thanks for taking this step. In closing, let this blessing precede you and follow you into the next week while you continue to marinate in God's Word:

May God light your path to greater understanding as you review the truths found in the books of the Minor Prophets and consider how they can help you grow closer to Christ.

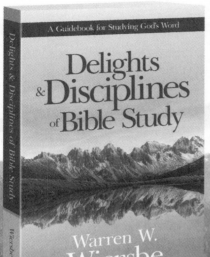